We Are Amused

We Are Amused

*Over 500 years of bons mots by
and about the Royal Family*

ALAN HAMILTON

ROBERT HALE · LONDON

Introduction and selection © Alan Hamilton 2003
First published in Great Britain 2003

ISBN 0 7090 7444 1

Robert Hale Limited
Clerkenwell House
Clerkenwell Green
London EC1R 0HT

A catalogue record for this book is available from the British Library

2 4 6 8 10 9 7 5 3 1

Printed by
St Edmundsbury Press Limited
and bound by
Woolnough Bookbinding Limited

Contents

Acknowledgements

The author is grateful to Sheil Land Associates for permission to quote from two collections of essays and speeches by HRH Prince Philip, Duke of Edinburgh: *Men, Machines and Sacred Cows* (Hamish Hamilton, 1984); and *Down to Earth* (Collins, 1988).

Introduction:
The Sayings of Royalty

Kenneth Williams, the frightfully camp and outra-
geously funny stalwart of 1970s radio comedy and of
the peculiarly British 'Carry On' films, expressed it
neatly in his autobiography. 'The nice thing about
quotes,' he wrote, 'is that they give us a nodding
acquaintance with the originator, which is often
socially impressive.'

This collection, therefore, should provide a nodding
acquaintance with the most socially impressive originators in Britain: the Royal Family. But quotations are not a
universally admired commodity. D.H. Lawrence wrote
to Aldous Huxley in 1928, roundly condemning their use
in literature: 'Nothing but old fags and cabbage stumps
of quotations – stewed in the juice of deliberate journal-
istic dirty-mindedness.' (He was, however, referring not
to royalty but to James Joyce – and Lawrence was a fine
one to talk about dirty-mindedness!)

What follows are the old fags and cabbage stumps
uttered over the years by the Royal Family: some of
them ancient but the overwhelming majority modern,
indeed thoroughly up-to-date. They have not been
stewed in the juice of dirty-mindedness – except,
perhaps, for a couple of secretly-taped lovers' telephone conversations which exploded across the tabloid
press in the 1990s to volcanic effect. Those are included

here as a matter of record, and with a nod to old Sam Johnson, who justified his dictionary of 1755 with the observation: 'Every quotation contributes something to the stability or enlargement of the language.' Had those telephone calls never made their way into the public prints, the English language would have been forever deprived of the word 'Squidgygate'.

The great majority of the quotations that follow owe their modest immortality to journalism, for they have appeared in newspapers, whether reported directly or indirectly. In many years at the coal face of royal reporting I have myself caught quite a few at first hand as they fell from the lips of their originators.

The ever-present danger of all quotations is that they are inevitably removed from their context. The constant complaint of public figures quoted in the media, especially in this sound-bite age, is that their remarks have been wrested from their roots and made to convey a meaning quite different to that intended. I believe, however, that all the quotations in this collection say what their originators meant them to say, and where the context is not immediately clear I have added brief explanations.

Ideally, quotations are distillations of thought, little gems of wit or wisdom, or windows of insight into character, behaviour and action. Few figures are as superficially familiar to us as the leading members of the Royal Family, yet they guard their innermost thoughts and opinions as though they were some intellectual Crown Jewels.

The Queen has never felt it necessary to unburden herself to a television chat show host, although she has offered occasional insights in serious television documentaries examining her role – notably in Edward

Mirzoeff's excellent film made for the BBC to mark her forty years on the throne. Her public speeches, once triumphs of the inoffensively anodyne, have grown sharper, wittier and perhaps even more heartfelt with age. Who could forget her rising to the microphone in the City of London Guildhall in 1992, her voice cracked with cold and the smoke of the Windsor Castle fire, to talk openly of her *annus horribilis*? In private she is jovial, funny and frighteningly well-informed – as I can personally testify. Fortunately for us, those who meet her and know her are occasionally indiscreet enough to pass on her pointed observations to a wider audience. (I shall not, however, disclose what she said about the canapés in Brisbane.)

Her husband is an entirely different matter. The Duke of Edinburgh has never been afraid to speak his mind and has enjoyed a long and illustrious career as the most vociferous and outspoken member of the Royal Family, the High Priest of political incorrectness. On the surface at least, he appears to be the master of the offensive aside, whether warning Scottish students in China that they are in danger of becoming slit-eyed, observing that some dubious electrical wiring looks as though it had been installed by Indians, or informing a blind woman with her guide dog that they now have eating dogs for anorexics.

The press loves these apparent blunders, and considers no state visit overseas to be complete without one of the Duke's 'gaffes'. The Duke, for his part, regards the tabloid press as being entirely without a sense of humour, and interested only in the raw material of punning headlines, like the *Daily Mirror*'s front-page masterpiece on the slit-eyed incident: 'The Great Wally of China'. He said that he embarked on every subsequent overseas visit in great trepidation, lest the British press were there. Invariably, they were.

He is self-deprecating enough to have admitted a talent for opening his mouth and putting his foot in it, even coining the word 'dentopedology' to describe the feat. But he is equally quick to defend himself. In the stiff formality of a royal visit, when those being visited are generally in a high state of nervousness, what is needed is an icebreaker. And there is no better reliever of tension than a joke, preferably laddish, unexpected and slightly inappropriate; it allows the royal personage to step down from his pedestal and shows that, after all, he is really rather human.

But Prince Philip is a paradoxical character. As well as being the most jocular member of the Royal Family, he is also perhaps the most philosophical. (Conversion from the Greek Orthodox faith of his birth to the Anglican of his wife must have spurred him to contemplate the nature of God.) He was one of the first high-profile public figures to take up cudgels on behalf of the future of the planet; he was campaigning on environmental issues long before it was a fashionable topic of debate, and certainly well before his eldest son adopted sustainable farming as his *cause célèbre*. Philip has never regarded himself as an expert in any particular field, but rather as a banger-together of heads, a facilitator and a source of common sense. A number of his deeper thoughts are included in this collection.

The Prince of Wales would also like to be regarded as a philosopher, but he is a blunderbuss to his father's rifle. He sprays his thoughts over a wide variety of targets, be they modern architecture, holistic medicine, the need to embrace Islam, the decline of Shakespeare in schools, organic farming, genetically-modified crops, or whatever. He is roundly abused for ill-informed meddling by the entrenched professionals in the fields he chooses to assault, and it is sometimes difficult to find a common thread in his pronouncements. If there is one, it is that we have lost the spiritual dimension to our lives – that we have become obsessed with building a better microchip when we should be devoting more energy and thought to living at one with Nature. As a broad philosophy, it is of course impossible to contradict; argument is over means, not the end, and many of Charles's targets regard his thinking as, at best, muddled. He does, however, sweeten the pill with an occasional dose of self-mockery – particularly since his tongue-in-cheek remark that he talked to his plants was swallowed whole by the tabloids.

There are a number of remarks that the Prince must now wish he had never uttered. His confession of adultery in the middle of an otherwise worthy television documentary in 1994 now seems in hindsight like the result of thoroughly bad advice from those whose job was to protect him. Its outcome was to draw a blistering counter-offensive from the Princess of Wales on the BBC's flagship current affairs programme *Panorama*; a record audience of 23 million tuned in to hear her talk of her 'crowded' marriage. Conducting a marital breakdown through rival television channels was a particularly unedifying exercise which damaged reputations all round, but what was said will be long remembered.

Certainly the observations made by the Princess that night were the most memorable utterances of her tragically short life. She was no philosopher, and happily described herself as both pea-brained and as thick as a plank. Her talents lay elsewhere, and she made enough observations in her time to remind us of her legacy of concern for the homeless, those dying of unfashionable diseases, and for the victims of landmines.

Her one-time partner in crime, the Duchess of York, is no philosopher either, but despite occasional bad behaviour with men to whom she was not married, she has always been rather endearingly frank, perhaps more so than she sometimes intended. She is highly popular in the United States as a cheerleader for the national obsession of losing weight, and there was hope that, as her career as a television presenter developed, she would become increasingly quotable.

There could hardly be two more different royal characters than the Duchess of York and the Princess Royal, the former the daughter of a rather louche old cavalry officer, and the latter (in the words of one waspish author quoted in this collection) Prince Philip in skirts. Princess Anne does not crack a great many jokes in public but when she does you get the feeling that you had damned well better laugh at them, or else. She harbours an abiding loathing and mistrust of the media. One photographer, a thoroughly charming lady and the daughter of a distinguished war cameraman, once accompanied the Princess as the sole journalist on a three-week tour of Central Asia; she returned complaining that never once on the whole tour had her quarry even bid her good morning.

The airy-fairy notions of her elder brother are anathema to the Princess, who is not above challenging his views on genetically-modified crops, forcefully and in public. She has been a long-serving and admired president of Save the Children, but she has never brought an ounce of sentimentality to the job. As she says in this collection, cuddling hungry children to please the cameras will bring no benefit to the children. You can see immediately why she and the Princess of Wales never got on; Diana would comfort patients dying of AIDS, whereas Anne dismissed the disease as a classic own-goal by the human race.

She is the first to admit she is anything but a fairytale princess, and proves it by telling a woman well-wisher who had travelled 50 miles to Sandringham to present a posy of flowers that it was 'a ridiculous thing to do'. She exudes the air, not of a princess, but of a high-powered international businesswoman. She is thoroughly practical. As President of the Missions to Seamen, she offered the thought that people often get carried away with what they imagined other people needed; what seamen far from home needed was 'a telephone, a drink, communication, company'.

Like so many other members of the Royal Family, Anne has had her marital difficulties. But you could not in your wildest dreams imagine her going on television to confess the intimacies of her private life. She maintains her dignity along with her brusqueness.

No member of the Royal Family in recent times maintained their dignity quite so well as Queen Elizabeth the Queen Mother; this she achieved largely by never giving an interview. (That is not quite true; she invited a reporter round at the time of her engagement in 1923, but told him absolutely nothing and merely invited him to admire her ring.)

During her public life, however, she made many speeches, often promoting the cause of women in society, and during the war she made several memorable morale-boosting broadcasts. Many of her more private observations have reached a wider world

because in her long widowhood she surrounded herself
with companionable and gossipy men – many of them
homosexuals of a certain age. Lord Wyatt of Weeford, a
former Labour politician, was not one of the latter, but
he was a member of her close circle, and his diaries are
occasionally revealing about their lunch-table conversations.

Born in the last year of Queen Victoria's life, she was
our last true Edwardian lady, and she brought into the
beginning of the twenty-first century the attitudes and
outlook of those distant times. She loved National Hunt
racing and a steady and generous supply of drink; it
was entirely typical of her to be found at the races with
her Thermos flask filled with champagne. Her *bête
noire*, on the other hand, was Mrs Wallis Simpson,
whose association with Edward VIII ultimately brought
Elizabeth's husband unwillingly to the throne in 1936.

It has always been generally assumed that Elizabeth
hated Wallis, and certainly there was never any
evidence of warmth between the two women, as a
quotation from Wallis in this collection reveals. But
many years after the event Elizabeth stated that she had
never hated Wallis; she had merely felt sorry for her.
More revealing, perhaps, is a handwritten letter from
her husband George VI, recently released after 66 years
hidden in the Public Record Office, telling his exiled
brother in France that George's wife and mother (Queen
Elizabeth and Queen Mary) had no wish to meet Wallis,
so a proposed trip by her and her husband to England
was a waste of time and had better be called off.

The Duke and Duchess of Windsor – as the ex-king
and his wife became after the Abdication – have always
been suspected of strong Nazi sympathies: one of the
underlying reasons why the 1936 Conservative govern-

ment of Stanley Baldwin was more than happy to be rid of its flawed monarch. But quotations from the Duke included here suggest that the case was probably somewhat overstated. At worst he was an appeaser of Hitler, having experienced the horrors of the all-too-recent Great War, not wishing Europe to be devastated again, and believing that Stalinist Russia, not Nazi Germany, was the real threat. Many people thought that way in the late 1930s.

Fortunately for subsequent history, King George VI and Winston Churchill did not. Nor did Queen Elizabeth; her letter (quoted here) to Lord Halifax, the foreign secretary, after reading Hitler's *Mein Kampf*, is illuminating. Equally enlightening is her much-quoted remark to a police constable after German bombs had scored a direct hit on Buckingham Palace: 'It makes me feel I can look the East End in the face.' It is a reminder that the Queen, so often portrayed as the shining heroine of victims of the Blitz on the London docklands, was not always so. On early visits to see the extensive bomb damage, she and the King were booed by the homeless victims of Hitler's raids; it was all right for them with their array of fancy houses, said the luckless Londoners.

Taking the Queen Mother's public life as a whole, however, she must be seen as a consummate actress who avoided controversy and always said the right thing. In old age she became a national institution, protected from criticism and demolition as though she were a valuable historic building. Even left-wing Labour MPs who made parliamentary careers out of attacking the waste and irrelevance of keeping a Royal Family at public expense almost universally excluded the Queen Mother from their vitriol.

Opponents of the Royal Family have been vociferous throughout the present Queen's reign, although their target has generally been the institution rather than the individual. The former Lord Altrincham, better known as the respected historian John Grigg, was an exception; as early as 1957 he published, in a learned and worthy periodical, a stinging criticism of the young monarch's personal style, which he found unbearably stuffy and artificial. Grigg was anything but an anti-monarchist, and his comments were intended to save the Queen from her own unimaginative courtiers, still pickled in the aspic of the pre-war era. But they caused the most frightful hullabaloo, and Grigg was so excoriated by the old guard of upper-class British society that he felt it necessary to renounce his hereditary title and his seat in the House of Lords. He was, of course, right all along. He recalled being warmly greeted by the Queen's private secretary some years later and profusely thanked for lighting his penny banger, exploding much of the court fustiness that would have sat ill with the approaching decade of the Swinging Sixties.

The Queen has moved with the times, as have her younger sons Andrew and Edward, both of whom have pursued careers in the real world. The Duke of York has expressed pertinent thoughts on his experience as a front-line helicopter pilot in the 1982 Falklands conflict (and on his previous role as a heart-throb), while his brother the Earl of Wessex has frequently been provoked into justifying, or apologizing for, his unconventional career, which had a false start in the Royal Marines, brushed with the huge egos of the theatre, and proceeded to swimming with the sharks in the dangerous pond of independent film production.

His wife the Countess of Wessex has yet to assemble a substantial canon of memorable sayings. Apart from a spirited public affirmation of her husband's heterosexuality, her modest contribution to this collection comes mainly from her comments to a robed sheikh she took to be a potential Arab client for her public relations company, but who was in truth a disguised Sunday newspaper reporter.

Nor have the Queen's grandchildren yet delivered their full quota of Socratic eloquence; they are too young, and they have quite rightly been largely excused public exposure as they complete their education. But they too occasionally live in the real world, where their utterances on being confronted by the hoipolloi have not always been quite up to the standard of an ancient Athenian academy.

Finally, there is Princess Michael of Kent, the daughter of an Austrian count, who, when she married Prince Michael in 1978 was regarded by the Queen as 'far too grand for the likes of us'. Being a haughty, noisy, ambitious outsider, the Princess always gives good value, because she has never fully embraced the British sense of discretion. Long may she speak.

A century from now, only a handful of quotations in this collection are likely to be jostling for space with snippets from the Bible and Shakespeare, Kipling and Churchill, whose jewels of perception and rhetoric fill the pages of weightier dictionaries that pour from the presses of Oxford and elsewhere. But there is nothing wrong with catching and preserving the mayflies of literature along with the mammoths – and some do survive the centuries. There is no more eloquent, apposite and currently relevant anti-smoking treatise than King James I's *Counterblaste to Tobacco*, written in a rage in 1604. It is not always true, as the American wit Robert Benchley claimed in 1936, that the surest way to make a monkey of a man is to quote him.

What Royalty Said

Henry VIII

———— ❧ ————

I am very sorry to know and hear how unreverently that most precious jewel, the Word of God, is disputed, rhymed, sung and jangled in every ale-house and tavern, contrary to the true meaning and doctrine of the same.

Address to Parliament, 1545

Elizabeth I

———— ❧ ————

The use of the sea and air is common to all; neither can a title to the ocean belong to any people or private persons, forasmuch as neither nature nor public use and custom permit any possession thereof.

To the Spanish Ambassador, 1580

If I am to disclose to you what I should prefer if I followed the inclination of my nature, it is: Beggar woman and single, far rather than Queen and married.

Quoted by Christopher Hibbert in *The Virgin Queen*, 1992

I know I have the body of a weak and feeble woman, but I have the heart and stomach of a king, and of a king of England too; and think it foul scorn that Parma or Spain, or any prince of Europe should dare to invade the borders of my realm.

> Speech at Tilbury on the approach of the Spanish Armada, 1588

The daughter of debate, that eke discord doth sow.

> On her cousin Mary, Queen of Scots, before ordering her execution, 1587

I am no lover of pompous title, but only desire that my name may be recorded in a line or two, which shall briefly express my name, my virginity, the years of my reign, the reformation of religion under it, and my preservation of peace.

> To her courtiers, discussing her epitaph

Though God hath raised me high, yet this I count the glory of my crown: that I have reigned with your loves.

> The 'Golden Speech', 1601

Although I may not be a lioness, I am a lion's cub, and inherit many of his qualities.

> On her father Henry VIII

I should call the wedding ring the yoke-ring.

> Her view on marriage

Alack, the Queen of Scots is lighter of a bonny son, and I am but barren stock.

> On the birth to her cousin Mary of the future James VI of Scotland and I of England, 1566

My lord, I had forgot the fart.

> To the Earl of Oxford, on his return from seven years' self-imposed exile after the embarrassment of breaking wind in the Queen's presence. (Quoted by the diarist John Aubrey)

James VI and I

The state of monarchy is the supremest thing upon earth; for kings are not only God's lieutenants upon earth, and sit upon God's throne, but even by God himself they are called gods.

> Speech to Parliament, 1609, justifying his belief in the Divine Right of Kings

It is a custom loathsome to the eye, hateful to the nose, harmful to the brain, dangerous to the lungs, and in the black stinking fume thereof nearest resembling the horrible Stygian smoke of the pit that is bottomless.

A Counterblaste to Tobacco, 1604, against Sir Walter Raleigh's successful efforts to popularize tobacco smoking

And for the vanities committed in this filthy custom, is it not both great vanity and uncleanness, that at the table, a place of respect, of cleanliness, of modesty, men should not be ashamed, to sit tossing of tobacco pipes and puffing of smoke and tobacco one to another, making the filthy smoke and stink thereof, to exhale athwart the dishes and infect the air, when very often, men that abhor it are at their repast? Surely smoke becomes a kitchen far better than a dining chamber, and yet it makes a kitchen also oftentimes in the inward parts of men, soiling and infecting them, with an unctuous and oily kind of soot, as hath been found in some great tobacco takers, that after their death were opened.

Ibid.

Such is the force of that natural self-love as we cannot be content unless we imitate everything that our fellows do, and so prove our selves capable of everything whereof they are capable, like apes, counterfeiting the manners of others, to our own destruction.

Ibid.

It is an iniquity that the husband shall not be ashamed, to reduce thereby his delicate, wholesome and clean complexioned wife to that extremity that either she must also corrupt her sweet breath there with, or else resolve to live in a perpetual stinking torment.

Ibid.

Charles I

Never make a defence or apology before you be accused.

Letter to Lord Wentworth, 1636

For the people truly I desire their liberty and freedom as much as anybody whatsoever; but I must tell you that their liberty and freedom consists in having government, those laws by which their lives and goods may be most their own. It is not their having a share in the government; that is nothing appertaining to them; a subject and sovereign are clean different things.

Awaiting his execution, 1649

I go from a corruptible crown to an incorruptible crown where no disturbance can be, no disturbance in the world.

His last words on the scaffold at Whitehall

Charles II

Let not poor Nelly starve.

Concern on his deathbed, 1685, for his mistress Nell Gwynne

George II

Oh! He is mad, is he? Then I hope he will bite some of my other generals.

On being told that General James Wolfe, who took Canada from the French, 1759, was a madman

George III

America is lost! Must we fall beneath the blow?

Letter bemoaning the loss of the colonies, 1782

It is to be hoped we shall reap more advantages from their trade as friends than ever we could derive from them as Colonies.

> *Ibid.*

I was the last to consent to the separation, but the separation having been made and having become inevitable, I have always said that I would be the first to meet the friendship of the United States as an independent power.

> Receiving John Adams, first American ambassador to London, 1785 (Adams subsequently become the second President of the US)

I that am born a gentleman shall never lay my head on my last pillow in peace and quiet so long as I remember the loss of my American colonies.

> In the early stages of his madness, 1788

George IV

'Harris, I am not well; pray get me a glass of brandy.

> To his manservant, on catching first sight of his bride-to-be, the dowdy and overweight Caroline of Brunswick, 1795

My Maria Fitzherbert is my wife in the eyes of God, and is and ever will be such in mine.

> On his mistress Mrs Fitzherbert, with whom he made an illegal marriage, written after his legal wife Caroline had given birth to a daughter, 1796

Pursued by the factions which divide my country and by the hostility of the greatest European powers, I have ended my political career and I come, as Themistocles did, to seat myself at the hearth of the British people. I put myself under the protection of its laws, which I claim from Your Royal Highness as the strongest, most consistent and most generous of my foes.

> Napoleon's appeal to the Prince Regent for political asylum in England after his defeat at Waterloo, 1815

Upon my soul, a very proper letter – much more so, I must say, than any I ever received from Louis XVIII.

> The Prince Regent's reaction

Queen Victoria

———<>———

We are not amused.

> (Attrib.) Said to have been uttered when she caught a
> courtier performing an impersonation of her, 1900

Great events make me quiet and calm; it is only trifles
that irritate my nerves.

> Letter to King Leopold of the Belgians, 1848

The Queen is most anxious to enlist every one who can
speak or write to join in checking this mad, wicked
folly of 'Woman's Rights' with all its attendant horrors,
on which her poor feeble sex is bent, forgetting every
sense of womanly feeling and propriety. Feminists
ought to get a good whipping. Were women to 'unsex'
themselves by claiming equality with men, they would
become the most hateful, heathen and disgusting
of beings and would surely perish without male
protection.

> Expressing her dismay at the suffragette movement
> campaigning for women to have the vote, 1870

Being pregnant is an occupational hazard of being a
wife.

> Awaiting the birth of her ninth and last child, 1857

An ugly baby is a very nasty object, and the prettiest is frightful when undressed.

> Letter to her daughter the Princess Royal, 1859

He speaks to me as if I was a public meeting.

> On her prime minister W.E. Gladstone

To me 'the people's William' is a most disagreeable person half-crazy.

> Further dislike of William Gladstone, 1873

I am sick of all this horrid business – of politics and Europe in general, and think you will hear some day of my going with the children to live in Australia, and to think of Europe as of the moon.

> Letter to her daughter the Princess Royal, 1860

I regret exceedingly not to be a man and to be able to fight in the war. There is no finer death for a man than on the battlefield.

> On the outbreak of the Crimean War, 1854

A happy New Year to my kind friend, from his true and
devoted one.

Christmas card to John Brown, 1878

I have lost my dearest best friend who no-one in this
world can ever replace.

On the death of John Brown, 1883

I would venture to warn against too great intimacy with
artists, as it is very seductive and a little dangerous.

Letter to her daughter Victoria, 1878

We are not interested in the possibilities of defeat. They
do not exist.

On the outbreak of the Boer War, 1899

Edward VII

Gentlemen, you may smoke.

> To his courtiers on ascending the throne, 1901 (Queen
> Victoria had banned smoking at court)

I cannot be indifferent to the assassination of a member of
my profession. We should be obliged to shut up business
if we, the Kings, were to consider the assassination of
Kings as of no consequence at all.

> On the murder of King Alexander of Yugoslavia, 1903

George V

Today 23 years ago dear Grandmama died. I wonder
what she would have thought of a Labour Government.

> His diary entry when he invited Ramsay Macdonald to
> form Britain's first Labour government, 1924

Few things are more earnestly desired throughout the English-speaking world than a satisfactory solution of the age-long Irish problems, which for generations embarrassed our forefathers, as they now weigh heavily upon us.

> Speech at the inauguration of the Northern Ireland parliament, Belfast, 1921

I may be uninspiring, but I'll be damned if I'm alien.

> Retort after pro-republican novelist H.G. Wells had criticised his 'alien and uninspiring' court, 1917

After I am dead, the boy will ruin himself in twelve months.

> On his eldest son, the future Edward VIII, in whom he had little confidence, said to prime minister Stanley Baldwin

I pray to God that my eldest son will never marry and have children, and that nothing will come between Bertie and Lilibet and the throne.

> Said to Mabel, Countess of Airlie, at his Silver Jubilee ball, 1935, when he saw the future Edward VIII dancing with Mrs Wallis Simpson. His wish was fulfilled

Bugger Bognor.

> (Attrib.) His response to a suggestion during his last illness that a visit to the English seaside resort of Bognor Regis might benefit his health

Edward VIII

Something should be done.

Viewing poverty amongst unemployed Welsh miners, 1936

You must believe me when I tell you that I have found it impossible to carry the heavy burden of responsibility and to discharge my duty as King as I would wish to do without the help and support of the woman I love.

His abdication broadcast, 1936

If it had been hard to give up the Throne, it had been even harder to give up my country. I knew now that I was irretrievably on my own. The drawbridges were going up behind me. But of one thing I was certain: so far as I was concerned love had triumphed over the exigencies of politics.

On sailing into exile, 1936. From his 1951 memoirs, *A King's Story*

Remembering your courtesy and our meeting two years ago, I address to you my entirely personal, simple though very earnest appeal for your utmost influence towards a peaceful solution of the present problems.

Telegram to Hitler on the invasion of Poland, 1939

In spite of Hitler's phenomenal sway over the German masses, their Fuhrer struck me as a somewhat ridiculous figure, with his theatrical posturings and his bombastic pretensions.

His 1951 memoirs, *A King's Story*

Intuitively I felt that another great war in Europe was all too probable; and I saw but too clearly that it could only bring needless human suffering and a resurgent Bolshevism pouring into the vacuum of a ravaged and exhausted continent.

Ibid. on Hitler's occupation of the Rhineland

It would be a tragic thing if Hitler was overthrown.

Interview with *Liberty* magazine, USA, 1941. (He later claimed the words were put into his mouth by his American interviewer Fulton Oursler.)

You cannot kill 80 million Germans and, since they want Hitler, how can you force them into a revolution they don't want?

Ibid.

I could wish indeed that Your Royal Highness would seek advice before making public statements of this kind.

Prime minister Winston Churchill on publication of the *Liberty* interview

I never intended, nor would I ever have agreed, to renounce my native land or my right to return to it – for all time.

> Letter from France, 1937, to Prime Minister Neville Chamberlain on being told that a condition of financial support from his brother George VI was that he never set foot in England again without the King's permission

The financial condition is both unfair and intolerable, as it would be tantamount to my accepting payment for remaining in exile.

> *Ibid.*

It is hardly necessary for me to repeat to you my loyalty to my brother as King; nor as a patriotic English man could I countenance any disruptive action in others. But I cannot refrain from saying, with the frankness you would expect of me, that the treatment which has been meted out to my wife and myself since last December, both by the Royal Family and by the Government, has caused us acute pain.

> *Ibid.*

I need hardly tell you as an Englishman how distasteful voluntary residence in a foreign country without a defined object can be.

> Another letter to Chamberlain, who had advised the Duke against making a visit to England, 1938.

The Duchess of Windsor

You can never be too rich or too thin.

> Mrs Wallis Simpson on how she wooed and won the King

I was left with the distinct impression that, while the Duke of York was sold on the American station wagon, the Duchess was not sold on David's other American interest.

> Accompanying Edward VIII to show off a new car to the Yorks, later George VI and Queen Elizabeth, 1936

George VI

All right.
  Bertie.

> Coded telegram to inform his father that Lady Elizabeth
> Bowes Lyon had accepted his proposal of marriage, 1923

I never felt any fear of shells or anything else. It seems curious, but all sense of danger and everything else goes except the one longing to deal death in every possible way to the enemy.

> Recalling his time as a young midshipman at the Battle of
> Jutland, 1916

I never wanted this to happen. I'm quite unprepared for it. David has been trained for it all his life, whereas I've never seen a State paper. I'm a naval officer. It's the only thing I know.

> On taking the throne after the abdication of his elder
> brother David, Edward VIII, 1936

As I turned after leaving the Coronation Chair I was brought up all standing, owing to one of the bishops treading on my robe. I had to tell him to get off it pretty sharply as I nearly fell down.

> On his coronation, 1937

I think you know that neither the Queen nor Queen Mary have any desire to meet the Duchess of Windsor, and therefore any visit made for the purpose of introducing her to members of the Royal Family obviously becomes impossible.

> Letter to Prime Minister Neville Chamberlain, 1938, making clear the royal opposition to a visit to England planned by the Windsors

I have noticed a great improvement in my talking and also in making speeches, which I did this week. I'm sure I'm going to get quite all right in time, but 24 years of talking in the wrong way cannot be cured in a month. I wish I could have found him before, as now that I know the right way to breathe my fear of talking will vanish.

> On being treated for his stammer by Australian speech therapist Lionel Logue, 1926

We feel in our hearts that we are fighting against wickedness, and this conviction will give us strength from day to day to persevere until victory is assured.

> Christmas broadcast, 1939

I think of you, my peoples, as one great family, for that is how we are learning to live. We all belong to each other. We all need each other. It is in serving each other and in sacrificing for our common good that we are finding our true life. In that spirit we shall win the war, and in that same spirit we shall win for the world after the war a true and lasting peace. The greatness of any nation is in the spirit of its people. So it has always been since history began; so it shall be with us.

Christmas broadcast, 1941

The Queen and I have been overcome by everybody's kindness. We have only tried to do our duty during these five and a half years.

Reaction to huge crowds outside Buckingham Palace on the announcement of victory in Europe, 1945

You used a knife on me. Now I'm going to use one on you.

Producing a sword to knight Sir James Learmonth, the surgeon who operated on him before his last illness, 1951

Queen Elizabeth the Queen Mother

I feel very happy but quite dazed. We hoped we were going to have a few days' peace first, but the cat is now completely out of the bag and there is no possibility of stuffing him back.

On the public announcement of her engagement to Prince Albert, Duke of York, 1923

If there have to be gentlemen waiting outside my bedroom door I hope it's someone we know.

On the birth of her first child, 1926, when by now-defunct custom Sir William Joynson-Hicks, the Home Secretary,

had to be present to verify the identity of a new potential
heiress to the throne

Every day I pray to God that he will see reason, and not
abandon his people.

> Letter to Queen Mary as Edward VIII prepared to abdi-
> cate, 1936

I can hardly now believe that we have been called to this
tremendous task and (I am writing to you quite inti-
mately) the curious thing is that we are not afraid. I feel
that God has enabled us to face the situation calmly.

> Letter to the Archbishop of Canterbury on her husband's
> accession, after his brother's abdication, 1936

I do not advise you to read it through or you might go
mad, and that would be a great pity. Even a skip through
gives one an idea of his mentality, ignorance and obvious
sincerity.

> On reading Hitler's autobiography, *Mein Kampf*, and
> passing it on to Lord Halifax, the Foreign Secretary, 1939

I shall not go down like the others.

> During revolver practice in case of German invasion,
> 1940, referring to other royal families who had fled the
> Nazi advance

I'm glad we've been bombed. It makes me feel I can look
the East End in the face.

> To a policeman when Buckingham Palace was bombed,
> 1940. On previous visits to the East End of London to

inspect bomb damage she had been received coolly by
Blitz victims who had lost their homes

Perhaps I can try. I'm rather good with dogs.

To a Blitz victim trying to rescue her dog from the
wreckage of her East End home, 1940

We do a lot of gardening at home. The King is good at the
digging and the weeding, while I concentrate on the seca-
teurs.

On her horticultural skills, practised even in wartime

The Princesses could never leave without me, and I could
not leave without the King. And, of course, the King will
never leave.

To a suggestion from the Canadian Government that
Princesses Elizabeth and Margaret should be evacuated
there for their own safety during the war

It is not our way in our dark days to turn for support to
others. But even had we been minded so to do, your instant
help would have forestalled us. The warmth and sympathy
of American generosity have touched beyond measure the
hearts of all of us living and fighting in these islands.

Broadcast to the USA, 1941, offering thanks for gifts of
food, clothing and medical supplies when Britain was
facing Germany alone

Yes I have. Have you?

To an American newspaper reporter who asked if she had
ever eaten Woolton Pie (a meatless and unappetising
wartime dish of carrots, parsnips and pastry), 1941

The people in our own lands are used to looking up to their King's representative – the Duchess of Windsor is looked upon as the 'lowest of the low'.

> Letter to Lord Lloyd, Colonial Secretary, on the appointment of the Duke of Windsor as governor of the Bahamas, 1940

I believe strongly that when future generations look back on this most terrible war they will recognise as one of its chief features the degree to which women were actively concerned in it. I do not think it is any exaggeration to say that, in this country, at any rate, the war could not have been won without their help. That is a thought which gives me pride as a woman.

> Address to London civil defence workers, 1944

Elizabeth gave us sparking plugs all through dinner.

> On her daughter's enthusiasm for her wartime training as an Army motor mechanic, 1944

My goodness, it's been cold at Buckingham Palace.

> Reflecting on the deprivations of five and a half years' war when it finally ended, 1945

I understand perfectly. We feel very much the same in Scotland too.

> To a veteran of the defeated Boer side in the South African War of 1899–1901, who said that, although he was pleased to meet her as she toured his country in 1947, he could never really forgive the English

Since I have landed in Quebec, I think we can say that I am a Canadian.

> To two Scots-Canadian old soldiers who asked her to settle their argument over whether she was Scottish or English, 1939

The knowledge of facts or events is of no value if the mind is insufficiently trained or self-disciplined to understand them, to pass judgement on them, and finally to act quickly, boldly and clearly upon that judgement. Therefore I would like to name the qualities which I believe we need as the three Ds – the elder brothers of the three Rs: first, discernment, the ability to judge between the false and the true, the essential and the unessential; second, decision, the power to turn judgement into action; and third, design, the art of giving practical form to a plan of action.

> Address to Queen's College, London University, on its centenary, 1948

All that is best in womanhood is needed today – gentleness and a ready sympathy, courage, hatred of cruelty, and an instinctive love for the young, the weak and the suffering. By your residence at Cambridge you can add to these natural endowments the grace of a well-trained mind, full of purpose, empty of prejudice. The torch of learning has been handed to you. Bring the light into your homes, which are the cradles of Christian citizenship, and shine it upon your children and all whom you meet.

> Address to the Senate of Cambridge University on receiving an honorary Doctorate of Law, 1948

One must feel gratitude for what has been, rather than distress for what is lost.

> On the death of King George VI, 1952

Throughout our married life we have tried, the King and I, to fulfil with all our hearts and all our strength the great task of service that was laid on us. My only wish now is that I may be allowed to continue the work we sought to do together.

> *Ibid.*

One thought how small and selfish is sorrow. But it bangs one about until one is senseless.

> To Edith Sitwell, who had sent her a book of poems to comfort her, 1952

We in Britain are perhaps too much disposed to judge American policy by the making of it, which frequently takes place in an atmosphere of considerable clatter. We do not always wait as confidently as we should for the final results, which are apt to be moderate, generous and wise. Similarly, people in the United States are inclined to misrepresent British policy, because we go about it in our own quite different way.

> Address on Anglo-American relations to the English Speaking Union, New York, 1954

I've taken this villa to get away from everything, but I don't expect I shall ever be able to get there.

> On buying the Castle of Mey, in the far north of Scotland, as a private retreat, 1953

This is how you do it – it's like opening a huge jar of sweets.

> Instructing 6-year-old Prince Charles on the royal wave

The chopper has changed my life as decisively as that of Anne Boleyn.

> On helicopters, which became her favourite mode of transport after her first flight at Biggin Hill, Kent, 1955

Is that wise? You know you have to reign all afternoon.

> (Attrib.) To her daughter the Queen, who asked for a second glass of wine at lunch

Being Scots, I love France as all my countrymen have done.

> On a visit to Paris, 1956

That's racing, I suppose.

> To jockey Dick Francis, who was within yards of winning the 1956 Grand National on her horse Devon Loch when it mysteriously collapsed

I'm sorry to say my grandson has been rather fond of soccer.

> On being presented with a rugby ball for Prince Charles during a visit to Rugby School, 1961

There is all the difference in the world between the patient's meaning of the word and the surgeon's.

> On a medical bulletin stating that she was 'comfortable' after major abdominal surgery at King Edward VII Hospital, London, 1966

You must never look at your feet; my mother taught me that.

> Advice on how to appear in public

It's much more important not to miss anyone than to be five minutes late.

> Advice on meeting people

It's one of my little treats.

> On being discovered at the races with her Thermos flask filled with champagne

Don't worry; I've got my pearls to keep me warm.

> (Attrib). To the Queen, who saw her mother on television at Cheltenham races without a coat on a particularly cold day

What ho!
Elizabeth R.

Signing a letter of greeting to the P.G.Wodehouse Society

I do think it's so good that we've joined the [European] community, don't you? We can teach them so much, can't we?

To prime minister James Callaghan, 1976

The salmon's revenge.

When she was rushed to hospital with a fish bone stuck in her throat, 1981. She was a keen and experienced angler

Of course I was upset at the time, but I would never demean myself to hate her. I don't think I've ever hated anyone.

On the Duchess of Windsor, said to guests at a lunch, 1985

I like the dear old Labour Party.

Remark to former Labour MP Woodrow Wyatt, 1987

We are very vulnerable, and it is rather fraught having the gossip writers at you the whole time.

On newspaper reports of a marital rift between the Prince and Princess of Wales, 1987

Turn down the sound. When you're not present it's like hearing the Lord's Prayer while playing Canasta.

> To a servant, on hearing the National Anthem being played on television

Don't worry at all, don't apologize. It's marvellous – I've been able to watch *Dad's Army* right through from start to finish.

> To the Countess of Longford, who arrived an hour late for a dinner party

I don't have a problem with people not curtsying, but what worries me about Mrs Blair is that you can hear her knees locking.

> To author P.D. James on the new Prime Minister's wife, 1997

Hands off! That's mine.

> To George Carey, Archbishop of Canterbury, who mistakenly picked up her wine glass to toast her at a lunch to celebrate her hundredth birthday at City of London Guildhall, 2000

We are only young once, Crawfie; we want her to have a good time.

> To governess Marion Crawford, who was concerned at Princess Margaret's regular late nights out

The Queen

Lilibet.

>   Her name for herself before she could pronounce 'Elizabeth'

Grandpapa England.

>   Her childhood name for George V, seeing his portrait on the coinage

People here need bicycles.

>   Aged 10, on moving into Buckingham Palace, with its endless corridors, at her father's accession in 1936

When Mummy was crowned and all the peeresses put on their coronets it looked wonderful to see arms and coronets hovering in the air and then the arms disappear as if by magic …What struck me as being rather odd was that Grannie did not remember much of her own

Coronation. I should have thought that it would have stayed in her mind for ever.

> Her own account of her parents' Coronation, 1937

At the end the service got rather boring, as it was all prayers. Grannie and I were looking to see how many more pages to the end, and we turned one more and then I pointed to the word at the bottom of the page and it said 'Finis'. We both smiled at each other and turned back to the service.

> *Ibid.*

Your handkerchief is to wave, not to cry into.

> Admonishing Princess Margaret as their parents left for a tour of North America, 1939

My sister is by my side, and we are both going to say goodnight to you. Come on, Margaret.

> Wartime broadcast to America, 1940

If you see someone with a funny hat, Margaret, you must *not* point at it and laugh. And you must *not* be in too much of a hurry to get through the crowds to the tea table. That's not polite either.

> Teenage advice to her younger sister on how to behave at garden parties

I declare before you all that my whole life, whether it be long or short, shall be devoted to your service, and the service of our great imperial family to which we all belong. But I shall not have the strength to carry out this resolution alone unless you join in with me, which I now invite you to do. I know that your support will be unfailingly given.

> Broadcast from Cape Town on her twenty-first birthday, 1947

My corgis have become pram-minded. They pay more attention to the pram than me. They know it means a walk.

> On the birth of Princess Anne, 1950

Look, they've sent the hearses.

> On seeing the line of black official cars waiting at Heathrow as she returned from Kenya on the death of her father, 1952

My own name, Elizabeth, of course.

> Asked by her private secretary, Lord Charteris, what she
> wanted to be called as Queen, 1952

Much was asked of my father in personal sacrifice and
endeavour, often in the face of illness. His courage in
overcoming it endeared him to everybody. He shirked no
task, however difficult, and to the end he never faltered
in his duty.

> Tribute to King George VI on his death, 1952

Get me started.

> A plea for a push when she found her train dragging on
> the carpet as she walked up the aisle of Westminster
> Abbey to her Coronation, 1953

Yes, the crown does get rather heavy.

> To Cecil Beaton, taking the official Coronation photo-
> graphs, 1953, on the Imperial State Crown which weighs
> nearly three pounds

I'm not going to come out of my cabin until he is in a
better temper; I'm going to sit here on my bed until he's
better.

> To a courtier after a row with her husband on board the
> royal yacht *Britannia*, as told to author Robert Lacey

I don't think they knew who we were.

> On being greeted by her children on her return from a

six-month Commonwealth tour with the Duke of
Edinburgh, 1954

Do you want a dukedom or anything like that?

> To Winston Churchill on his retirement as Prime Minister,
> 1955. He politely declined

It is inevitable I should seem a remote figure to you.

> Her first Christmas television broadcast, 1957

If I were to cancel now, Nkrumah might invite
Khrushchev instead and they wouldn't like that, would
they?

> Brushing aside foreign office advice that because of civil
> unrest she should decline an invitation to make a state
> visit to President Kwame Nkrumah of Ghana, who was
> being courted by the Soviet Union, 1961

It's most unfortunate that all my sons have such long
eyelashes while my daughter hasn't any at all.

> To photographer Cecil Beaton on the birth of her fourth
> and last child Prince Edward, 1964

Back a bit, Ron; they've come to see me, not you.

> To Major Ronald Ferguson, then a senior officer in the
> Household Cavalry, riding too close to the Queen in a
> procession, 1964

I am not a film star.

> To Princess Anne, who urged her mother to join the miniskirt era, 1968

It is as Queen of Canada that I am here – Queen of Canada and all Canadians, not just one or two ancestral strains.

> Address in Ottawa, 1973, at the height of the French-Canadian Quebec separatist movement

Dog leads cost money.

> To Prince Charles, who took her dogs for a walk at Sandringham and returned without the lead

Keep your cameras trained; you may see the biggest walkout of all time.

> To photographers covering her disastrous state visit to Morocco, 1980, when King Hassan kept her waiting for two hours in a suffocating desert tent

Oh come on; get a bloody move on.

> To a policeman who, after a long delay, arrived to arrest intruder Michael Fagan, who found his way into her Buckingham Palace bedroom as she slept and asked her for a cigarette, 1982

In a way I didn't have an apprenticeship. My father died much too young, and so it was all a very sudden kind of taking on and making the best job you can.

> To BBC documentary director Edward Mirzoeff, 1983

Sandringham is an escape place. But it's also a working place and a commercially viable bit of England.

> *Ibid*. On the fact that her Norfolk estate makes a profit from farming

Sometimes it is worth explaining that we put it on specially; we do not actually live like this all the time.

> *Ibid*. On bringing out the best china and gold plate for visiting heads of state

I think people need pats on the back sometimes. It's a very dingy world otherwise.

> *Ibid*. On investitures and the honours system

I do rather begrudge some of the hours I have to do instead of being outdoors.

> *Ibid*. On the never-ending duty of having to read state papers

To be able to sleep in the same bed for six weeks is a nice change.

> *Ibid*. On summer holidays at Balmoral

It's rather nice to feel that one's a sort of sponge. Everybody can come and tell one things; some things stay there, some things go out the other ear, and some things never come out at all.

> *Ibid.* On the confidential weekly audiences with her prime ministers

If you live in this sort of life, which people don't very much, you live very much by tradition and continuity. I find that's one of the sad things, that people don't take on jobs for life; they try different things all the time.

> *Ibid.* On her job

I think this is what the younger members find difficult – the regimented side.

> *Ibid.* On the waywardness of the young royals

The training is the answer to a great many things. You can do a lot if you are properly trained, and I hope I have been.

> *Ibid.* On how she copes with her role

Please take a picture, someone, or no one will believe I'm here.

> On the Great Wall of China during her state visit to Beijing, 1986. Elspeth Howe, wife of the Foreign Secretary, obliged

If it weren't for my Archbishop of Canterbury I should be off in my plane to Longchamps every Sunday.

> On her love of racing

Have we been watching too much *Edward and Mrs Simpson*, do you think, Mr Fox?

> To her milliner who proposed a thirties-style hat in 1988, when the BBC was showing a popular dramatization of the Abdication story

I'm not a model girl. I don't want clothes to pose in.

> To her dress designer Ian Thomas

It's extraordinary. My mother doesn't need glasses at all and here I am 52 ... 56 – well, whatever age I am – and can't see a thing.

> On producing a pair of spectacles for the first time to read a speech, 1982

One plants one's feet apart like this. Always keep them parallel. Make sure your weight is evenly distributed. That's all there is to it.

> Advice to Susan Crosland, wife of the Foreign Secretary, on the secret of standing for hours

Ask a silly question ...

> Visiting a cattle breeding centre in East Anglia, after asking what a particular piece of equipment was, and being told it was an artificial vagina

I've decided that I'm not stuffy enough for my age.

> Signalling her equanimity at the news that Princess Anne had separated from her husband Captain Mark Phillips and taken up with her equerry, Commander Tim Laurence, 1989

I know all about noise. I live at the end of an airport runway.

> On the serious noise pollution at Windsor Castle

Nineteen ninety-two is not a year I shall look back on with undiluted pleasure. In the words of one of my more sympathetic correspondents, it has turned out to be an *annus horribilis*.

> Speech at a City of London Guildhall lunch to mark her forty years on the throne, 1992, days after a disastrous fire at Windsor Castle

No institution – City, monarchy, whatever – should expect to be free from the scrutiny of those who give it their loyalty and support, not to mention those who don't. This sort of questioning can also act, and so it should do, as an effective agent of change.

> *Ibid.*

Fine, let's go. Stop mucking around.

> On being told by her private secretary Sir Robert Fellowes that she would have to start paying income tax, 1992

You know, democracy takes a long time.

> To reformist Russian President Boris Yeltsin on the first state visit to Moscow since the Bolshevik Revolution, 1994

We all felt the shock and sorrow of Diana's death. Thousands upon thousands of you expressed your grief most poignantly in the wonderful flowers and messages left in tribute to her. That was a great comfort to all those close to her.

Christmas broadcast, 1997

Recent developments at home, which have allowed Scotland and Wales greater say in the way they are governed, should be seen in that light and as proof that the Kingdom can still enjoy all the benefits of remaining united.

Ibid.

I know that, despite the huge constitutional difference between a hereditary monarchy and an elected government, in reality the gulf is not so wide. They are complementary institutions, each with its own role to play. And each, in its different way, exists only with the support and consent of the people.

Speech at lunch given by Prime Minister Tony Blair to mark her golden wedding anniversary, 1997

That consent, or lack of it, is expressed for you, Prime Minister, through the ballot box. It is a tough, even brutal, system but at least the message is a clear one for all to read. For us, a Royal Family, however, the message is often harder to read, obscured as it can be by deference, rhetoric or the conflicting currents of public opinion. But read it we must. I have done my best, with Prince Philip's constant love and help, to interpret it correctly through the years of our marriage and of my reign as your Queen. And we shall, as a family, together try to do so in the future.

Ibid. In response to calls for the Royal Family to learn from the down-to-earth informality of the late Princess Diana

Prime Minister, I know that you, like your predecessors, will always pass such messages, as you read them, without fear or favour.

Ibid.

All too often, I fear, Prince Philip has had to listen to me speaking. Frequently we have discussed my impending speech beforehand and, as you will imagine, his views have been expressed in a forthright manner. He is someone who doesn't take easily to compliments but he has, quite simply, been my strength and stay all these years, and I, and his whole family, and this and many other countries, owe him a debt greater than he would ever claim or we shall ever know.

Ibid.

For goodness sake, don't let Mummy have another drink.

Instruction to a pageboy serving at a reception attended by the Queen Mother

I have always made it clear that the future of the monarchy in Australia is an issue for you, the Australian people, and you alone to decide by democratic and constitutional means. It should not be otherwise.

> Speech in Sydney, 2000, after the country had voted narrowly in a referendum not to become a republic

It's not as difficult as it might seem. You see, I don't have to introduce myself; they all seem to know who I am.

> To an MP who sympathized with her on having to meet so many strangers

Following the tragic events of September 11 all of us, whatever our religion or background, have an added responsibility to ensure that those who are intent on stirring up hatred, fear and prejudice in this country do not succeed.

> Speech at a banquet for King Abdullah of Jordan, 2001

They stiffen but they do not curtsy.

> Observation on Cherie Blair's knees, 2001

I didn't realize the whole family were here.

> Viewing a display of creepers, spiders and strangely-shaped vegetables at the Chelsea Flower Show, 2001

How are your feet?

> On knighting Olympic gold medallist Sir Steven Redgrave after he had run in the London Marathon, 2001

The doctors say that I have chickenpox quite mildly for a grown-up, but it is not much consolation when one is covered in spots.

> Letter written to Prime Minister Edward Heath in 1971, released by the Public Record Office, 2002

As a people, Scots like to argue principle. Quite properly, there has been some strong debate within this Parliament and close scrutiny of its contribution from without.

> Golden Jubilee address to the Scottish Parliament, Aberdeen, 2002

Yours is a society which has given so much to the world. I particularly value your commitment to community, to learning, to the spirit of enterprise and to equality of opportunity for all.

> *Ibid.*

I am more than conscious at the moment of the importance of football. Although this weekend comes about half way through my Jubilee year, as far as we are concerned it bears no relation to a rest at half-time.

> Golden Jubilee address at City of London Guildhall, as England scored some early successes in the World Cup in Japan, 2002

It has been a pretty remarkable 50 years by any standards.

> *Ibid.*

The Duke of Edinburgh has made an invaluable contribution to my life over these past fifty years, as he has to so many charities and organizations with which he has been involved. We both of us have a special place in our hearts for our children. I want to express my admiration for the Prince of Wales and for all he has achieved for this country. Our children, and all my family, have given me such love and unstinting help over the years, and especially in recent months.

> *Ibid*. Both her mother and sister died at the beginning of her Jubilee year

Gratitude, respect and pride; these words sum up how I feel about the people of this country and the Commonwealth – and what this Golden Jubilee means to me.

> *Ibid*.

Which direction is Mecca?

> On her first visit to a British mosque, at Scunthorpe, Lincolnshire, 2002

The dreadful attacks of September 11 may have threatened freedom, innocence and other values we hold dear, but they also inspired grace, charity and courage.

> Message to New York on the first anniversary of the Twin Towers, 2002

I've decided I'm not old-fashioned enough to be Queen.

> Reflecting on populist – and popular – celebrations for the Golden Jubilee, 2002

I would like above all to declare my resolve to continue, with the support of my family, to serve the people of this great nation of ours to the best of my ability through the changing times ahead.

> Jubilee address to both Houses of Parliament, dismissing speculation that she might abdicate, 2002

We are a moderate, pragmatic people, more comfortable with practice than theory. With an offshore, seafaring tradition, we are outward-looking and open-minded, well suited by temperament and language to our shrinking world.

> *Ibid.*

We are inventive and creative – think of the record of British inventions over the past fifty years or our present thriving arts scene. We also take pride in our tradition of fairness and tolerance; the consolidation of our richly multicultural and multifaith society, a major development since 1952, is being achieved remarkably peacefully and with much goodwill.

> *Ibid.*

If one were going to be interviewed by anyone, it wouldn't be you.

> To John Humphrys, presenter of the BBC Radio 4 *Today* programme, at a reception for the media, Windsor Castle, 2002

I was just putting on my tiara when the lights went out.

> On a power cut as she was dressing for a state dinner in Kingston, Jamaica, 2002

None of my governments seem to know what to do about them.

> (Attrib.) In a discussion on recessions, with another one looming, 2002

You'd better answer that; you never know, it could be somebody important.

> To an embarrassed Jubilee garden party guest whose mobile phone went off just as she was being introduced to the Queen, 2002

You have given a lot of women a lot of pleasure.

> On meeting popular television gardener Alan Titchmarsh, 2002

Getting lots of reading practice in my childhood stood me in good stead, because I read very quickly now. I have to read a lot.

> Complimenting author J.K. Rowling on her Harry Potter books

That was interesting.

> On being stranded for half an hour in freezing conditions on a broken-down water taxi ferrying her across a river in Winnipeg, 2002

Do they fight?

> To members of the Manitoba Welsh Corgi Association
> who brought their dogs along to show the Queen in
> Winnipeg, implying that her own pack may still be less
> than perfectly behaved

How very reassuring.

> To a fellow-shopper in Sandringham village store, who
> had remarked to the woman she did not recognize that
> she looked awfully like the Queen

There are powers at work in this country about which we
have no knowledge.

> (Attrib.) To former royal butler Paul Burrell, whose trial
> collapsed in 2002 when the Queen suddenly remembered
> she had had a conversation with him

We'll go quietly.

> Her stock response whenever the question of a republican
> Britain is raised

The Duke of Edinburgh

A discredited Balkan prince of no particular merit or
distinction.

> On himself.

An uncultured polo-playing clot. I'm one of those stupid bums who never went to university, and I don't think it's done me any harm.

> On himself

The difference between a free society and one in which all issues are governed by inflexible dogma is the constant exchange of ideas.

> Introduction to his book *Men, Machines and Sacred Cows*, 1984

It makes me an amoeba – a bloody amoeba.

> On the Queen's decision that their children should take the name of Windsor, and not Mountbatten. She subsequently changed her mind

Judging by the amount of time and space given to such things as the national economy, the balance of payments, the size of the GNP, the Public Sector Borrowing Requirement and the figures of unemployment, you would think that they were all more important than people.

Essay, 'People are People', 1984

It is not the national economy which decides the circumstances of the individual, it is the other way round. Governments can control such things as the rate of public spending, the rate of taxation and hence the rate of inflation. They can lay down the rules governing industrial, commercial and professional enterprise, but the state of the economy is decided by the way people respond to these conditions. The Government cannot order rates of enterprise, creativity, productivity or profitability; these are decided by people.

Ibid.

Within 150 years we have progressed from horse-drawn and wind-blown transport to machines which can fly passengers at twice the speed of sound. But people go on in much the same way. The only difference between highwaymen and hijackers is that the latter use politics as a justification.

Ibid.

A life devoid of challenge or risk, an existence of total stability and total security, may be splendid for cabbages but it would not be much fun for people.

Ibid.

It is not what people are forced to do by law, it is what they want to do by conviction that decides the state of civilization in which they are going to live.

Ibid.

There is no difference between a crooked lawyer and a dishonest social worker. A thief is a thief whether he is a professor or an undergraduate.

Ibid.

One of the consequences of our complex modern way of life which makes things so difficult for individuals is the apparent necessity for people to be surveyed, recorded, numbered, pigeon-holed, and above all put into categories. Everybody has to be divided up into classes and occupations, workers and managers, income, ethnic and age groups, and any number of others, including of course the 'don't knows' who figure so largely in opinion polls. Yet for human purposes they are all totally irrelevant. If you come to think of it, there are really only two categories of people, the good and the bad or the decent and the indecent.

Ibid.

I doubt I've achieved anything likely to be remembered.

On himself

Wives play an extremely important part in polo and many promising young players have had the terrible choice of keeping their ponies or keeping their wife. Some lucky ones somehow manage to persuade their wives to keep, groom and train their ponies, but this ideal arrangement is understandably rare.

On the high cost of his favourite game

I declare this thing open whatever it is.

On a visit to Canada, 1969

It seems to me that the people of this world are facing the same dilemma as the man on the desert island. He has a coconut tree, which provides him with food, but he has decided to cut it down to build a shelter. He is very comfortable in his shelter but he has just begun to notice that his store of coconuts is beginning to run out.

Lecture to the European Council of International Schools, 1986

It's a pleasant change to be in a country that isn't ruled by its people.

> On a visit to Alfredo Stroessner, dictator of Paraguay, 1969

Constitutionally I don't exist.

> On the fact that there is no official role for the husband of a reigning monarch

I must confess that I am interested in leisure in the same way that a poor man is interested in money. I can't get enough of it. Furthermore, I have no problem whatever in filling my leisure time and I worry not at all whether what I do is good or wise or likely to improve my character or to help me become a 'whole man'.

> Essay on leisure, 1984

People are inclined to make bland statements about the duty of individuals to develop their talents to the full. This is all very laudable, but say that to an adolescent and you might as well tell a blind man to see red.

> *Ibid.*

I have no sympathy with people who claim to know what is good for others. My contention is that no one should be prevented from taking part in any reasonable activity through ignorance or lack of facilities and no one should be forced into crime because it is the conventional thing to do.

> *Ibid.*

Here comes the chain gang.

> On the approach of the mayor and councillors to
> welcome him on a visit to Nottingham

You must sometimes stretch out your neck, but not actually give them the axe.

> On his own highly opinionated views

I could use any one of several stock phrases or platitudes, but I prefer one I picked up during the war. Gentlemen, I think it is time we pulled our fingers out.

> Address to the Industrial Co-Partnership Association on
> Britain's inefficient industries, 1961

We all know only too well that city people have always maintained a rather patronizing air of superiority over the bumbling and old-fashioned farmer. I am not going to suggest that city people are totally lacking in intelligence so I can only assume that this superiority is due to simple ignorance. The fact of the matter is that farmers in the technologically advanced countries have progressed just as fast as any other industry.

> Address to the Royal Agricultural Society of the
> Commonwealth, 1967

Oh well, I suppose I can always turn it into a flower pot.

> On being presented with yet another stetson hat during a
> tour of Canada

Does that mean there will be a twenty-five-year interval between trains?

On London Transport's choice of name for the Jubilee Line

One of the evident characteristics of computers is that, so far at least, they are unencumbered with any kind of emotion or aesthetic judgement. Their great advantage is that their responses are, or are at least intended to be, entirely rational, whether they are engaged in playing games, recognizing features, correcting grammar or translating from the Chinese. They do not get angry if they are asked silly questions and they do not make guesses if they do not know the answer. Neither are they liable to any prejudice that is not programmed into them.

Essay, 'On Being in Two Minds', 1984

Cheer up sweetie, give them a smile.

To the Queen, looking glum at an official engagement

It is a complete misconception to imagine that the monarchy exists in the interests of the Monarch. It doesn't. It exists in the interests of the people.

> Answering left-wing criticism of the cost of keeping the monarchy

To make any comment about human population is just about as dangerous as going for a Sunday afternoon walk in a minefield. I do believe, however, that human population pressure – the sheer number of people on this planet – is the single most important cause of the degradation of the natural environment, of the progressive extinction of wild species of plants and animals, and the destabilization of the world's climatic and atmospheric systems.

> Lecture to the Commons All-Party Group on Population and Development, 1987

How does a girl get a mink? The same way a mink gets a mink.

> Another view of the population explosion

Are you asking me when the Queen is going to die?

> On being asked when Prince Charles would succeed to the throne

If it has got four legs and it is not a chair, if it has got two wings and it flies but is not an aeroplane, and if it swims and is not a submarine, the Cantonese will eat it.

> Address on endangered species to the World Wildlife Fund, 1986

No society that values its liberty can do without the freedom to report on, comment on, discuss and indeed to gossip about people, institutions and events. I have yet to come across a Society, free or otherwise, that seems to be short of volunteers to make speeches, give lectures, write for the press, perform for radio or television, or, if all else fails, to write letters to the editor. Some do it for a living, others do it because they feel the need to complain, enlighten, inform or persuade their fellow citizens, and there are some who do it because they are invited. The flattery of the invitation is usually enough to overcome any fear or reluctance to accept. Talent is seldom a serious consideration.

Essay, 'Prejudice, Malice and Sacred Cows', 1984

Anyone who puts pen to paper or voice on tape for public consumption is bound to include something of his or her own personality. It is probably a determination to be totally impersonal, and hence hopefully untraceable, that drives bureaucrats to compose their material in gobbledygook.

Ibid.

Sacred cows thrive on being taken seriously; they cannot stand being laughed at.

Ibid.

The almost universal reaction to an incomprehensible idea is to ignore it, presumably in the hope that it will go away. When Captain Cook pulled the *Endeavour* up on a beach on the Australian coast in order to effect repairs, he noticed that some native fishermen, not far away, continued their activities without even looking around at what must have been the equivalent of the landing of a flying saucer.

Ibid.

It is not really a question of whether they are legal or illegal, but whether it is sensible or not.

His view on drugs

Surely we've had enough. If he's not got what he wants by now he's an even worse photographer than I think he is.

Impatience at the time taken by Cecil Beaton over a family photograph

I can't help wondering if we are really justified in our attempts to solve African problems. I just wonder how we would react, for instance, to African intervention in some of our social problems, such as drugs, crime, hooliganism and unemployment? Perhaps we ought to take

the beam out of our own eye before we bother about the speck in our brother's eye.

Address to the World Wildlife Fund, 1985

When a man opens a car door for his wife, it's either a new car or a new wife.

On the etiquette of marriage

At least they don't break if you drop them.

On the gold plates used at state banquets

It is interesting that Marx, who was largely responsible for one of the utopian egalitarian systems, did not really object to the wildly unequal feudal system, because he maintained that under it everyone had their rights and responsibilities. It was, in his view, the irresponsible exercise of power and private wealth by the bourgeois capitalists that caused all the trouble. Unfortunately his solution has proved to be worse than the original problem.

Essay, 'People and Systems', 1984

The most intractable problem for even the best-intentioned systems occurs when people acquire a vested interest in keeping them as they are.

Ibid.

Everybody was saying we must have more leisure; now they are complaining that they're unemployed.

On Britain's economic recession, 1981

The biggest waste of water in the country by far. You spend half a pint and flush two gallons.

> On the environmental disadvantage of lavatories

It's like saying adultery is all right as long as you don't enjoy it.

> To an anti-hunt demonstrator who confessed to eating meat

I don't see the difference between eating wild animals killed by myself and domestic animals killed by a professional in an abattoir. I shoot the surplus of a wild population and make sure that I leave enough to breed another surplus next year. This may be a moral issue for some. It is certainly not a conservation issue. The danger is taking more than can be replaced. This applies to fish in the sea and trees in the forest.

> On his devotion to game shooting

I'm in a bit of a quandary this evening because I can't very well talk about charity all the time. In which case I'm left with the press and, quite frankly, I'd rather be left with a baby.

> Proposing the toast to the Newspaper Press Fund, a journalists' charity

If the man had succeeding in abducting Anne, she would have given him a hell of a time while in captivity.

> On a gunman who tried to kidnap Princess Anne from her car, 1974

The apparently obvious solution to a problem is seldom, if ever, the right solution. One very good reason for this is that problems are never as straightforward as they appear to be at first sight. Furthermore, in the real world, neither the problems nor their solutions bear any obvious relationship to what the theorists and ideologists believe them to be.

Essay, 'Subsidies, Price Controls and Grants', 1984

The most persistent and universal problem is that of human poverty and the discovery of its solution. Merely putting the blame on to another group in society or on to some system or other has never come near to finding a solution.

Ibid.

I look after it for him while he's at school.

Caught by the Queen playing with Prince Charles's electric train set

Judging by the comments on the tyranny of the telephone and the tirades of the prophets of doom on the subject of television, there are obviously some who feel that, like Christopher Columbus, Marconi went rather too far.

Essay on 'Communication,' 1984

We are rapidly approaching the time when almost anything is possible. Existing knowledge and techniques are such that the only limit to scientific progress and material development is the human capacity to think up new ideas.

Ibid.

Without the chance of receiving the message of religious thought, the most well-meaning, energetic and intelligent human is really no more than a bumble-bee trapped in a bottle.

On his spirituality

The inexorable laws of nature dictate that any species can only expand to the point at which its numbers threaten the health and productivity of its own habitat. The more it destroys its habitat, the more certain it is that it will destroy itself.

Down To Earth, collected environmental speeches, 1988

The biggest animal with the smallest brain.

His definition of a horse

I hope he breaks his bloody neck.

> When a photographer covering his visit to India fell out of a tree

They're just people who wait around for the moment when you pick your nose to take a photograph of you.

> On photographers in general

Wildlife, whether in the shape of birds, animals, fish or plants, is being threatened and eroded as never before in history. If we do not get the answer right now, there will not be a second chance, and this, our generation, will go down in history as the people who failed by neglect and indifference to take decisive control of our environment for the benefit of our successors in the future. Of course we may all be dead by the time the full horror of our neglect becomes apparent, but I for one do not relish the idea of my grandchildren asking me what went wrong.

> Address to the Canadian Audubon Society, 1967

You have mosquitoes: we have the press.

> On a visit to the Caribbean island of Dominica

The World Wildlife Fund was only founded less than twenty-five years ago, yet you may recall that Noah started it all umpteen thousand years ago with his ark. Even then he was presumably too late to save the dinosaurs, unless there were several arks.

> Speech to the Council for Environmental Conservation, 1982

The trouble with anything to do with horses is that, by the time you have discovered all the problems and risks, it is too late to be of any practical use.

Essay, 'Horses are Horses', 1984

The difference with Noah is that he was saving the animals from a disaster deliberately organized by the Almighty against the unruly and sinful human population. Conservationists today are trying to save them from a human-created disaster, not from just a single flood but from two revolutions and an explosion. The industrial revolution, the scientific revolution and the human population explosion.

Ibid.

There are cases already within the Common Market where ancient and long-standing agricultural patterns have been completely up-ended as a result of the operation of the Common Market system in Europe.

Speech to the Royal Agricultural Society of the Commonwealth, 1971, for which he was forced to apologize to a British Government locked in delicate negotiations for Common Market membership

I am afraid the mere words 'Common Market' have the same effect on the press as the bells had on Pavlov's dogs.

His letter of apology to Prime Minister Edward Heath

If you travel as much as we do, you appreciate how much more comfortable aircraft have become – unless you have to travel in something called economy class, which sounds ghastly.

Visiting the Aircraft Research Association, Bedfordshire, 2002

You look like a suicide bomber.

To a female armed police officer, Stornoway, Isle of Lewis, 2002

Do you know they're now producing eating dogs for anorexics?

To a blind woman with a guide dog in a crowd outside Exeter Cathedral, 2002

Yak yak yak: come on, get a move on.

Shouted from the deck of Britannia in Belize, 1994, to the Queen who would not stop chatting to her hosts on the quayside

The development of military weapons and techniques between wars is always a bit uncertain because the difference between what people think is going to happen in war and what actually happens increases in direct proportion to the interval between wars. It is further complicated by what some people would like to happen in war.

> Centenary address to the Royal Aeronautical Society, 1966

You're too fat to be an astronaut.

> To Andrew Adams, 13, who had expressed an ambition to go into space, Salford, 2001

Prince Philip wishes to make it clear that at no point did he ever use the insulting terms described in media reports.

> Buckingham Palace statement, 2002, refuting claims that he had written letters to Diana, Princess of Wales, calling her 'a trollop and a harlot'

Because she is the sovereign everyone turns to her. If you have a king and queen, there are certain things people automatically go to the queen about. But if the queen is also the Queen, they go to her about everything. She is asked to do much more than she would normally.

> On his wife's role, 1994

We don't do this for fun, you know; we do it because people want us to come.

> During a gruelling tour of Canada, 1984

Do you people still throw spears at each other?

> To a distinguished group of Aboriginal community leaders, Queensland, 2002

Technology marches on but it leaves in its wake polluted seas and rivers, polluted air, polluted land and polluted food. I do not think it is fanciful to suggest that the birds and animals and fish which are dying in this process are equivalent to the miner's canary: the first warning that things are not quite right.

> Lecture to the Institute of Fuel, 1967

You'd better be jolly careful, or you'll come back slit-eyed.

> To a group of Edinburgh University undergraduates studying in Xian, China, 1986

You can't have been here very long; you haven't got a pot belly.

> To a British resident of Budapest, home of robust central European cuisine, 1993

That looks as though it was put in by an Indian.

> Pointing to a primitive fusebox in a Glasgow factory, 1998

The trouble with success is that it takes a long time before its unpleasant consequences become known.

> Address to the Engineering Industries Association, 1976

The age of social conscience, social justice and concern seems to have coincided with the age of crime, pornography, mugging, selfish indulgence and international terrorism. What started out as a liberalization of restrictive social conventions seems to have developed into a dictatorship of licence.

> Address to the Canadian Club, 1977

I suspect that what industrialism has done for mankind is to give it the impression that everything in the world from children's play to a housing estate can be planned and made to function with the efficiency of a nuclear power station. Whereas the real truth is that, whatever our material achievements, we are still human, and that it is the facts of human nature and not the binary system which must govern human affairs.

> *Ibid.*

It was always my impression that it was King Canute who first demonstrated that there were limitations to the effectiveness of government decrees.

> Address to the Tree Council, 1978

I can only assume that it is largely due to the accumulation of toasts to my health over the years that I am still enjoying a fairly satisfactory state of health and have reached such an unexpectedly great age.

> At a City of London Guildhall lunch to celebrate his eightieth birthday, 2001

Do not let us forget we have been genetically modifying animals and plants ever since people started selective breeding ... People are worried about genetically modified organisms getting into the natural environment. What people forget is that the introduction of exotic species – like, for instance, the introduction of the grey squirrel into this country – is going to do or has done far more damage than a genetically modified piece of potato.

> In defence of genetically modified foods, 2000

I am desperate if I find there are British press on a foreign visit. I know they'll wreck the thing if they possibly can.

> Interview with the *Sunday Telegraph*, 1999

The *Daily Express* is a bloody awful newspaper.

> Response to the paper's report that he had shouted 'Where's my bloody aeroplane?' at an airport

I don't think it's good for the brand image to have practically an octogenarian at the top. Inevitably, your faculties begin to fail as you get older. It's much better to go while you're still capable than wait till people say you're so doddery it's time you went.

> Interview with *Saga Magazine*, 1999, on handing over presidency of the Duke of Edinburgh's Award Scheme to the Earl of Wessex

I've become a caricature. There we are; I've just got to live with it.

> *Ibid.*

I think the main lesson we have learnt is that tolerance is the one essential ingredient (of marriage). It may not be quite so important when things are going well, but it is absolutely vital when the going gets difficult. You can take it from me that the Queen has the quality of tolerance in abundance.

> Lunch at City of London Guildhall to celebrate their golden wedding anniversary, 1997

I am, naturally, somewhat biased, but I think our children have all done rather well under very demanding circumstances and I hope I can be forgiven for feeling proud of them.

Ibid.

If a cricketer, for instance, suddenly decided to go into a school and batter a lot of people to death with a cricket bat, which he could do very easily, are you going to ban cricket bats? There's no evidence that people who use weapons for sport are any more dangerous than people who use golf clubs or tennis rackets or cricket bats.

Opposing a call for the banning of handguns after a shooting club member had killed a teacher and seventeen pupils at a school in Dunblane, Perthshire, 1995

How do you keep the natives off the booze long enough to get them past the test?

Meeting a driving instructor on a visit to Oban, Argyllshire, 1995

Where on earth do you keep your microphones?

To the scantily-clad cast of the musical *Chicago*, Adelphi Theatre, London, 1999

Her behaviour was a bit odd. But I'm not vindictive; I don't see her because I don't see much point.

On the Duchess of York, in a *Sunday Telegraph* interview, 1999

Deaf? If you're near there, no wonder you're deaf.

> To members of the British Deaf Association standing beside a steel band at Welsh Assembly celebrations, 1999

This is a lot less expensive than the Dome – and I think it will be a lot more useful.

> Opening a new mathematics centre at Cambridge University in Millennium year, 2000

Your country is one of the most notorious centres of trading in endangered species in the world.

> Accepting a conservation award in Thailand, 1991

Aren't most of you descended from pirates?

> Visiting the Cayman Islands, 1994

The bastards murdered half my family.

> Rejecting a suggestion that he might make an official visit to the Soviet Union, 1967

So *you're* responsible for the kind of crap that Channel Four produces.

> On meeting Sir Michael Bishop, chairman of Channel Four Television, 1996

I can't understand a word they say; they slur all their words.

> On French Canadians during a visit to Toronto, 1985

You bloody clots! You could take pictures like this any Sunday at home in Windsor, yet you come all the way to Jamaica to do it.

> To press photographers accompanying him on a West Indies tour, 1963

If it doesn't fart or eat hay, she's not interested.

> On Princess Anne's preferred choice of company

You look as if you're ready for bed.

> To the Nigerian secretary-general of the Commonwealth arriving for a meeting in his tribal robes

There's an awful lot of things that, if I were to re-read them now, I'd say to myself: 'Good God, I wish I hadn't said that.'

> On his own loquaciousness

All I'll say is that I've tried to keep it going while I've been here.

> Prince Philip on his role in the monarchy, 1999

The Prince of Wales

I know my mother is Queen, but how do I put that on the envelope?

> Writing his first letter home from Cheam school, 1957

I remember being acutely embarrassed when it was announced. I heard this marvellous great cheer coming from the stadium in Cardiff, and I think for a little boy of nine it was rather bewildering. All the others turned and looked at me in amazement.

> On hearing on the school radio that his mother had created him Prince of Wales, 1958

I gave up smoking at the age of eleven. I had one or two strong ones behind the chicken run at school.

> Reminiscences of Cheam School, 1998

I simply dread going to bed as I get hit all night long ... I can't stand being hit on the head by a pillow now ... It is hell here, especially at night.

> Letter home on being bullied at Gordonstoun school, 1962

There's hardly any religion, and you should see where we have to have church. It's a sort of hall which is used for films and assemblies and plays, sometimes for football or gymnastics. And then one is expected to worship in there. It's hopeless; there's no atmosphere of the mysterious that a church gives one.

> Letter from Gordonstoun on the school's pagan atmosphere

I thought, 'I can't bear this anymore,' and went off somewhere else. The only other place was the bar. Having never been into a bar before, the first thing I thought of doing was having a drink, of course. And being terrified, not knowing what to do, I said the first drink that came into my head, which happened to be cherry brandy, because I'd drunk it before when it was cold out shooting. Hardly had I taken a sip when the whole world exploded round my ears.

> His own account of an incident on a school expedition to Stornoway, Isle of Lewis, in 1963, when crowds peered through the window of a hotel where his party was sheltering from the rain. The story of his under-age drinking made headlines around the world

I had this schoolboy dream that I was going to escape and hide in the forest, in a place where no one could find me, so that I wouldn't have to go back to school. I hated that institution, just as I hated leaving home.

> Looking back on his Gordonstoun schooldays

In Australia you are judged on how people see you and feel about you. There are no assumptions. You have to fend for yourself.

> On the joy of two terms' escape to Geelong Grammar School, Melbourne, 1964

My most vivid memory of that day is of several burly, bowler-hatted gentlemen dragging shut those magnificent wooden gates to prevent the crowd from following in. It was like a scene from the French Revolution.

> On his arrival at Trinity College, Cambridge, 1966

The everlasting splashing of the Great Court fountain ... and the everlasting sound of photographers' boots ringing on the cobbles ... the grinding note of an Urban District Council dust lorry's engine rising and falling in spasmodic energy at seven o'clock in the morning, accompanied by the monotonous jovial dustman's refrain of 'O Come All Ye Faithful' and the headsplitting clang of the dustbins.

> Impressions of college life, 1968

It was a great challenge to climb over the wall. Half the fun of university life is breaking the rules.

> Regret at Trinity's decision to keep its front gate open later at night

I haven't many friends; there haven't been many parties.

> On his term at University College, Aberystwyth, to prepare for his investiture as Prince of Wales, 1969

I remember thinking what a very jolly and amusing and attractive 16-year-old she was. Great fun: bouncy and full of life.

> On the first casual encounter with Lady Diana Spencer, 1977

When you marry in my position, you're going to marry someone who, perhaps, is one day going to be Queen. You've got to choose somebody very carefully, I think, who could fulfil this particular role, and it has got to be somebody pretty unusual.

Interviewed on marriage, 1969

I wanted to give Diana a chance to think about it – to think if it all was going to be too awful.

On proposing to Diana just before she left for a holiday in Australia, 1981

It's only twelve years. Lots of people have got married with that sort of age difference. I just feel you're only as old as you think you are ... Diana will certainly keep me young. I think I shall be exhausted.

Television interview on the engagement, 1981

Whatever 'in love' means. Put your own interpretation on it.

Asked in the same interview if the couple were in love

Well, stand them further apart.

On being told the huge cost of providing enough servicemen to line his wedding procession route, 1981

Our wedding was quite extraordinary as far as we were concerned. It made us extraordinarily proud to be British.

On the vast crowds lining the route from St Paul's Cathedral to Buckingham Palace

She's not here, there's only me, so you'd better go and ask for your money back.

> On being eclipsed in popularity by his new wife, 1982

It was rather a grown-up thing. I found it rather a shock to my system.

> On being present at the birth of Prince William, 1982

On of the reasons I asked Sir Laurens Van der Post to be a godfather was because he is one of the best storytellers I have ever come across and I want my son to be able to sit on his godfather's knee and listen to his wonderful stories.

> Sir Laurens, writer, Jungian philosopher and sometime guru to Charles, was regarded by some critics as something of a sham

I'm sorry he's not all that smiley today. They never do what you want them to. We'll probably get all those child specialists saying we handled him wrong.

> On William at six months

I wouldn't have missed being present when William and Harry were born. Husbands who turn up later only see a baby which might have been picked off a supermarket shelf for all they know.

> On the joys of the delivery room, 1984

I would like to bring up our children to be well-mannered, to think of other people, to put themselves in other people's positions, to do unto others as they would have done unto them. At the end of it, even if they are not very bright or very qualified, at least if they have reasonable manners they will get much further in life than by not having them.

Criteria for parenthood, 1984

I never thought it would end up like this. How could I have got it so wrong?

Letter to a friend on the disintegration of his marriage, 1986

Your great achievement is to love me.

To Camilla Parker Bowles in the 'Camillagate' taped telephone conversation, 1993

God forbid, a Tampax – just to live inside your trousers.

Ibid. Speculating on what he might come back as if reincarnated

Mrs Parker Bowles is a great friend of mine. She's been a friend for a very long time, and will continue to be for a very long time.

To TV interviewer Jonathan Dimbleby in the documentary *Charles: The Private Man, The Public Role*, 1994

Obviously I'd much rather it hadn't happened, and I'm sure my wife would have felt the same. It wasn't for lack of trying, you know, on both parts, trying to ensure these things work. I accept there is a certain amount of damage. I mean you can't avoid it with something of this unfortunate nature.

> *Ibid.* On his separation from Diana

Yes, absolutely. Yes, until it became irretrievably broken down, both of us having tried.

> *Ibid.* His public admission of adultery, when asked if he had tried to be 'faithful and honourable' to Diana when he took his marriage vows

I think those who marry into my family find it increasingly difficult to do so because of the added pressure. The strains and stresses become almost intolerable.

> *Ibid.*

That sort of thing is very much for the future. If it happens, then it will happen.

> *Ibid.* Asked if he was planning divorce

I feel very strongly about things. I don't see why politicians should think they have the monopoly of wisdom.

> *Ibid.*

Life is a more profound experience than we are told it is.

> Millennium message, 2000

I love coming in here, and I potter about and sit and read. I just come and talk to the plants really. Very important to talk to them; they respond, I find.

> Television interview in his Highgrove garden, 1986. Said with a laugh, but taken at face value by the tabloid press ever since

Only the other day I was inquiring of a whole bed of old-fashioned roses, forced to listen to my demented ramblings on the meaning of the universe, while sitting cross-legged in the lotus position on a gravel path in front of them, what would happen on my birthday in a Birmingham tram shed. The roses were aghast. Could they not find somewhere more salubrious? Apparently not, I told them; most of the rest of Birmingham had been knocked down.

> Address to a surprise fortieth birthday party staged for him by the Prince's Trust in a converted Birmingham tram depot, 1988

A row of prize Welsh leeks, cocky little things, chipped in to say that the shed would be filled with semi-naked Kalahari bushmen performing a fertility dance, together with several troupes of Tibetan Buddhist monks who had levitated from Saffron Walden. There would also be a whole flock of pedigree gurus telling me what to say to hovering groups of Buddhists. Don't be so ridiculous, I told them; they wouldn't dare. Oh yes they would, chorused half an acre of Brussels sprouts.

> *Ibid.*

It's really the result of talking to trees once too often.

> Wearing a patch over his left eye after getting sawdust in it, 2001

I believe agriculture has lost its soul. Organic farming can put its soul back.

> The Highgrove organic farmer, 1998

In this technology-driven age, it is all too easy for us to forget that mankind is part of nature and not apart from it, and that is why we should seek to work with the grain of nature in everything we do.

> Reith Lecture, BBC Radio 4, 2000

Some recent occurrences, such as the BSE disaster and perhaps – dare I mention it – the present severe weather conditions in our country, are, I have no doubt, the consequences of man's arrogant disregard of the delicate balance of Nature.

> Address to the British Medical Association, 2000

Since bees and the wind don't obey any sort of rules, we shall soon have an unprecedented and unethical situation in which one farmer's crop will contaminate another's against his will.

> Taking a strong stand against genetically modified crops, 1999

Genetically altered food crops take mankind into realms that belong to God, and to God alone.

Still campaigning, 2002

The sense of humanity's uniqueness is thrown out of the window to be replaced by an egocentric world view which denies that all-encompassing sense of the sacred, and stresses the purely rational.

An attack on modern architecture, 1992

I understand all the arguments about being contemporary and about the need to reflect the spirit of the age, but what alarms me is that the age has no spirit.

To American architects in Washington, 1990

Much of the commercial building of today bears as much relation to architecture as advertising slogans bear to literature.

Ibid.

While I am thoroughly in favour of the avant-garde generally, what I don't think is acceptable is when the avant-garde becomes the establishment.

His continuing war on ugliness, 1994

We used to have Nimbys, but now I am told we have a newer, even tougher generation known as Bananas: Build Absolutely Nothing Anywhere Near Anything.

On opponents of planning applications, even for buildings he would approve of, 1999

It seems like a clever way of building a nuclear power station in the middle of London without anyone objecting. I have tried hard to appreciate it but I can't, I can't.

ᘁ

On the National Theatre, South Bank

That is redolent of a word processor to me, and I don't see that people particularly want to live looking at a word processor when they have to live with them all the time.

On a City of London office block

I personally would go mad if I had to work in a place like that because I would feel how the hell do you get out in the event of a fire, apart from anything else?

On Britain's tallest building, the 800-foot tower at Canary Wharf, London Docklands

How can you even tell it's a library? It has no character to suggest it is a great public building. Its Reading Room looks more like an assembly hall of an academy of secret police.

ᘁ

On the new British Library at St Pancras, London

It looks rather like an old 1930s wireless. What on earth is the point of having conservation areas if we are going to disregard them?

On the Mansion House Square development, City of London

It looks like a place where books are incinerated, not stored.

On the new Central Library, Birmingham

Choosing my words to be as inoffensive as possible, I said I thought it was an unmitigated disaster.

On a proposed convention centre, Birmingham

A monstrous carbuncle on the face of an elegant and much-loved friend.

On a design for a proposed extension to the National Gallery, London. (It was discarded in favour of a more acceptable scheme.)

Please may there still be programmes which recognize that a large proportion of the population is in fact older, whose tastes and views may have developed to the point where it does not always want innovation and excitement all the time, but is sometimes looking for reliability, familiarity and continuity.

Address to the Royal Television Society, 2002

Throughout the twentieth century so much ancient, accumulated, traditional wisdom has been thrown away, whether in the fields of medicine, architecture, agriculture or education. The baby was thrown out with the bathwater.

Article on his 'Healing Garden' of medicinal plants and shrubs in catalogue for Chelsea Flower Show, 2002

Western medicine has tended to regard disease as a parcel of symptoms to be dosed or chipped out, losing sight of the whole person behind the rash or lump, and the various emotional and environmental factors that may contribute to their physical problems.

Ibid.

Health should be much more than the mere absence of disease or infirmity; and we should strive to ensure that everybody can fulfil the full potential and expression of their lives.

Article on homeopathy in the *Daily Telegraph*, 1997

These two worlds, the Islamic and the Western, are at something of a crossroads in their relations. We must not let them stand apart. I do not accept the argument that they are on course to clash in a new era of antagonism. I am utterly convinced that our two worlds have much to offer each other. We have much to do together.

Speech to the Oxford Centre for Islamic Studies, 1993

All the great prophets, all the great thinkers, all those who have achieved an awareness of the aspects of life which lie beneath the surface, all have shown the same understanding of the universe or the nature of God or of the purpose of our existence, and that is why I think it so important to understand the common threads which link us all in one great and important tapestry.

On understanding other religions, television interview, 1994

I personally would rather see it as Defender of Faith, not *The* Faith, because Defender of the Faith means just one particular interpretation of the Faith.

> *Ibid.* Discussing the title which links the sovereign to the Church of England

Everywhere in the world, people are seemingly wanting to learn English. But in the West, in turn, we need to be taught by Islamic teachers how to learn once again with our hearts as well as our heads.

> Speech to a conference of academics and religious leaders, Sussex, 1996

I find it almost incredible that in Shakespeare's land one child in seven leaves school functionally illiterate. There are terrible dangers, it seems to me, in so following fashionable trends in education towards the 'relevant', the exclusively contemporary, the immediately palatable, that we end up with an entire generation of culturally disinherited young people.

> Speech at Stratford on the 426th anniversary of Shakespeare's birth, 1991

I was asked in Australia whether I concentrated on improving my image – as if I was some kind of washing powder, presumably with special blue whitener. I dare say I could improve it by growing my hair to a more fashionable length, being seen at the Playboy Club at frequent intervals and squeezing myself into excruciatingly tight clothes. But I intend to go on being myself to the best of my ability.

> In defence of his un-hip image, 1982

I've got a long body and short legs. And please don't blame photographers for making my ears look large. They *are* large.

The noble art of self-deprecation

I hope you infants are enjoying your infancy as much as we adults are enjoying our adultery.

Joking to a group of schoolboys – before he was married

I was once elected one of the world's best-dressed men. The following year I was elected one of the worst-dressed. At a tailor's dinner just after that I decided to have my own back. I arrived wearing white tie and tails and an old tweed jacket over the top. The British are a wonderful race: they pretended I was normally dressed.

Ibid.

I am often asked whether it is because of some generic trait that I stand with my hands behind, like my father. The answer is that we both have the same tailor. He makes our sleeves so tight that we can't get our hands in front.

Ibid.

I find it quite a challenge being who I am.

Asked what had been his greatest challenge in life

I've only got to look twice at someone and the next morning I'm engaged to her.

On frantic press speculation on whom he might marry, 1978

Awkward, cantankerous, cynical, bloody-minded, at times intrusive, at times inaccurate and at times deeply unfair and harmful to individuals and to institutions.

His view of the press on the 300th anniversary of the founding of the *Daily Courant*, England's first daily newspaper, 2002

It has always been one of my profoundest regrets that I was not born ten years earlier than 1948, since I would have had the pure, unbounded joy of listening avidly to the Goons. I only discovered that Goon-type humour appealed to me with a hysterical totality just as the shows were drawing to a close.

On admitting that the *Goon Show*'s trademark 'Ying Tong Song' was the only song he knew by heart

I shall miss his irreverent and hysterical presence.

On the death of *Goon Show* creator Spike Milligan, 2002

He will be profoundly missed by all those people who appreciate wit and unmalicious humour. He was one of the great life-enhancers of our age.

> On the death of Sir Harry Secombe, another original Goon, 2001

What's your brother up to these days?

> On meeting Bakr bin Laden, brother of Osama, 2001

A man among men, a king among kings.

> Tribute to King Hussein of Jordan on his death, 1999

Above all she saw the funny side of life and we laughed until we cried – oh, how I shall miss her laugh and wonderful wisdom born of so much experience and an innate sensitivity to life. She was quite simply the most magical grandmother you could possibly have, and I was utterly devoted to her.

> Tribute on the death of Queen Elizabeth the Queen Mother, 2002

Your Majesty – Mummy. In my long experience of pop concerts this has been something very special indeed. I do not think any of us will ever forget this evening. We, Your Majesty, are here tonight because above all we feel proud of you.

> To the Queen at the Golden Jubilee pop concert, Buckingham Palace gardens, 2002

You have defended our laws and given us cause to shout a heartfelt *God Save the Queen*.

Ibid.

If we fail to understand that true sustainability depends on accepting certain limits to human ambition and working more in harmony with the mysterious processes of Nature, then we face a social and natural catastrophe of unimaginable proportion.

Accepting a French environmental award, Paris, 2003

Diana, Princess of Wales

I'll never marry unless I really love someone. If you're not really sure you love someone, then you might get divorced. I never want to be divorced.

As a teenager, mindful that her parents separated when she was six

I never got any O levels – always too busy. Brain the size of a pea, I've got.

On her undistinguished academic record at school

I actually wanted to be a dancer, but overshot the height by a long way.

On the drawbacks of being 5' 10" tall

Prince Charles came to stay as a friend in my sister's house for a shoot, and we sort of met in a ploughed field.

Recalling their first casual encounter in 1977

Pretty amazing.

Her first impression of the Prince of Wales

I haven't got a background. That's what everybody else seems to have. I mean I haven't had a *chance* to have a background like that. I'm only nineteen.

As she was being courted by Charles, 1980

Anyone in my situation would be feeling the pressure. However I'm still bearing up, in spite of all the attention surrounding me. I haven't been carted off yet. I'm still around. I'm getting to know the reporters. I feel sorry for them having to wait outside my flat in all weathers.

On being hounded day and night, 1980

You know I cannot say anything about the Prince or my feelings for him. I am saying that off my own bat. No one has told me to keep quiet. I'm sorry; it must be a real bore for you.

As good as confirmation of the romance, 1980

You see, my sister Sarah was going out with Charles last year. She talked to the press too much, I think, and they *murdered* her.

Ibid.

I was so nervous about the whole thing I never thought I'd be standing with the light behind me. I don't want to be remembered for not having worn a petticoat … I ended up in the papers with legs looking like a Steinway piano's.

> On a famously revealing backlit photo of her with the sun shining through her skirt, 1980

It wasn't a difficult decision. It was what I wanted – it is what I want.

> Interviewed on her engagement, 1981, on whether she had immediately accepted Charles's proposal

I can't get used to wearing it yet. The other day I even scratched my nose with it because it's so big – the ring I mean.

> On her engagement ring

I am absolutely delighted, thrilled, blissfully happy. I never had any doubts.

> Television interview on the eve of her wedding, 1981

I have the best mother-in-law in the world.

> On the Queen, 1981

Everybody is so *old* around here.

> Her initial reaction to courtiers at Buckingham Palace

It was as if he was married to them, not me, and they are so patronizing it drives me mad.

On Charles's own staff at St James's Palace

He is a doting daddy and does everything perfectly.

On her husband following the birth of Prince William, 1982

It was like a baptism of fire, but by the time I left I felt I'd actually been able to achieve something.

Accompanying Charles on her first official overseas tour, to Australia, 1983

Being a princess is not all it's cracked up to be ... imagine having to go to a wedding every day of your life – as the bride. Well, it's a bit like that.

Finding the Australian tour hard work, 1983

The trouble with being a princess is that it's so hard to have a pee.

Ah, so that's the drawback!

If men had to have babies they would only have one each.

On being pregnant, for a second time, with Prince Harry, 1984

I just can't understand how anyone can abandon their children. I love my own so much.

Visiting a Barnardo's children's home, 1985

Oh, you should have seen some of those Arabs going ga-ga when they saw me on the Gulf tour. I gave them the full treatment and they were just falling over themselves. Just turned it on and mopped them up.

> On the success of her official tour of Gulf states with Charles, 1986

Oh, it hasn't got any numbers. I couldn't manage a watch without numbers.

> Having second thoughts about a Cartier watch she fancied

I'd love to have my conk fixed. It's too big.

> Worries about her nose

I'm never on what is called a diet. Maybe I'm so scrawny because I take too much exercise. When I get home I just have to chase around for a chicken leg because I'm so busy.

> Said before it became widely known that she suffered from bulimia

When I wear a backless dress, I find that most people just don't know where to put their hands.

> On her role as a fashion icon

When we first got married we were everyone's idea of the world's most perfect, ideal couple. Now they say we're leading separate lives. The next thing I know I'll read in some newspaper that I've got a black lover.

> The first cracks appear, 1987

I always feel he will be all right because he has been born to his royal role. He will get accustomed to it gradually.

On Prince William, aged six

I was very bad at lunch and I nearly started blubbing. I just felt really sad and empty and thought 'Bloody hell, after all I've done for this f***ing family'.

Telephone call from Sandringham to James Gilbey, a car salesman, while she was staying with the Royal Family at Christmas, 1989, recorded and subsequently published as the 'Squidgygate' tape

I don't know how I would cope if I had a child who was handicapped or mentally handicapped in some way. So I'm going out there, meeting these children, and I'm learning all the time and trying to understand, trying desperately to understand how they cope.

On becoming President of Barnardo's, 1985

I'll bet you have some fun chasing the soap around the bath.

To a one-armed man at a Help the Aged home, 1986

I take my teddy to bed every night, and he travels with me everywhere I go.

To a 5-year-old patient in a Dorset hospital, 1988

These should be shown on television so everyone could see the damage smoking does.

On being shown slides of diseased lungs at the Brompton Hospital, 1986

After I had been round the first ward – I remember it so vividly – I was struck by the calmness of the patients in their beds in confronting their illness. They were so brave about it, and made me feel so humble.

On her first visit to a hospice, 1985

For me, one of the particularly sad things about my visits [to AIDS clinics] has been to find out how much stigma people with AIDS and HIV still suffer, and how much they feel they have to deal with prejudice as well as their physical problems.

On World AIDS Day, 1994

I've taken William and Harry to people dying of AIDS – albeit I told them it was cancer. I've taken the children to all sorts of areas where I'm not sure anyone of that age in this family has been before. And they have a knowledge. They may never use it, but the seed is there and I hope it will grow, because knowledge is power.

Panorama interview, 1995

A stable domestic background, where the simple duties of family life are shared and understood, can do much to strengthen those tempted to find a refuge in drink or drugs.

Address to Turning Point, a rehabilitation charity, 1989

When I've asked addicts why they became addicted, the most common reason is anger. Anger at their parents, anger at their schools, anger at their communities. In fact, anger at life in general.

Launching European Drug Prevention Week, 1992

Children are sometimes portrayed as problems to solve and not as souls to love and cherish. Children are not chores, they are part of us. If we gave them the love they deserve, they would not try so hard to attract our attention.

Ibid.

Hugging has no harmful side-effects. If we all play our part in making our children feel valued, the result will be tremendous; there are potential huggers in every family.

Ibid.

Touch my face; I don't mind at all.

To a blind man who met her during a hospital visit, 1995

There are two basic agents when defining us as human beings: one, a sharpness of mind; two, kindness of the heart – hearing and sharing the grief of others.

Receiving a Humanitarian of the Year award, 1995

When I started my public life 12 years ago, I understood that the media might be interested in what I did. I realized then that their attention would inevitably focus on both our public and private lives. But I was not aware how overwhelming that attention would become, nor the extent to which it would affect both my public duties and my personal life, in a manner that has been hard to bear.

> Announcing her partial withdrawal from public life, 1993, a year after the announcement of her marital separation

Over the next few months I will be seeking a more suitable way of combining a meaningful public role with, hopefully, a more private life.

> *Ibid.*

My first priority will continue to be our children, William and Harry, who deserve as much love, care and attention as I am able to give, as well as an appreciation of the tradition into which they were born. I would also like to add that this decision has been reached with the full understanding of the Queen and the Duke of Edinburgh, who have always shown me kindness and support.

> *Ibid.*

I hope you can find it in your hearts to understand and to give me the time and space that has been lacking in recent years.

> *Ibid.*

Homelessness is an experience which isn't confined to the festive season. It is not a problem that miraculously appears on the first day of Christmas and then disappears on the twelfth. It is a daily problem for many of our towns and cities.

Speech to Centrepoint, a charity for the homeless, 1996.

The age of homeless youngsters is coming down. Children as young as eleven called at Centrepoint this year.

Ibid.

Children need every chance available to help them along the difficult path to adulthood. A good education, a safe place to live and play, and someone who will listen are all essential ingredients of a decent start in life.

Foreword to Barnardo's annual report, 1996

Don't worry, I can't smell it; I had a Chinese meal last night.

To a patient in a Sheffield hospital who apologized for the strong aroma of liniment on his body, 1994

The waste of life, limb and land which anti-personnel mines are causing among some of the poorest people on earth is a waste of which our world is too unaware, for the mine is a stealthy killer long after the conflict is ended.

Campaigning against landmines, Washington, 1997

I have seen some horrifying things over the years, but I have learned to cope with it because each person is an individual, each person needs a bit if love. You don't think about yourself.

Visiting landmine victims in Angola, 1997

I have seen lots of poverty before but I have never seen such devastation.

> Visiting Sarajevo, Bosnia, on her anti-landmines campaign, 1997

Well, there were three of us in this marriage so it was a bit crowded.

> BBC *Panorama* interview, 1995

I think I've always been the 18-year old girl he got engaged to, so I don't think I've been given any credit for growth. And my goodness, I've had to grow.

> *Ibid.*

Anything good I ever did, nobody ever said a thing, never said 'well done' or 'was it OK?' But if I tripped up, which I invariably did because I was new at the game, a ton of bricks came down on me ... Obviously there were lots of tears, and one could dive into the bulimia, into escape.

> *Ibid.*

I desperately wanted it to work, I desperately loved my husband, and I wanted to share everything together, and I thought we were a very good team.

> *Ibid.*

I wasn't daunted, and am not daunted by the responsibilities that that role creates. It was a challenge; it is a challenge. As for becoming Queen, it was never at the forefront of my mind when I married my husband; it was a long way off, that thought.

Ibid.

The most daunting aspect was the media attention, because my husband and I were told when we got engaged that the media would go quietly, and it didn't. And then when we were married they said it would go quietly, and it didn't. And then it started to focus very much on me, and I seemed to be on the front page of a newspaper every single day, which is an isolating experience, and the higher the media put you, place you, the bigger the drop. And I was very aware of that.

Ibid.

The enemy was my husband's department because I always got more publicity. My work was discussed more, much more, than him.

Ibid.

Yes, I adored him. Yes, I was in love with him. But I was very let down.

Ibid. On her relationship with James Hewitt

My wish is that my husband finds peace of mind, and from that other things follow, yes.

Ibid. Asked if it was her wish that Prince William rather than the Prince of Wales should succeed the Queen

Nothing brings me more happiness than trying to help the most vulnerable people in society. It is a goal and an essential part of my life – a kind of destiny. Whoever is in distress can call on me. I will come running, wherever they are.

> Interview with French newspaper *Le Monde* shortly before her death, 1997

You will have a big surprise coming soon, at the next thing I do.

> Tantalizing remark to photographers during a holiday as guest of Mohammed al-Fayed in St Tropez, two weeks before her death, 1997. Thought to be an allusion to her romance with Hasnat Khan, a Pakistani heart surgeon

Prince William

She would have known that constant reminders of her death can create nothing but pain to those she has left behind.

> Joint statement with Prince Harry on the first anniversary of their mother's death, 1998

I wanted to see the world and help people.

> On why he joined an Operation Raleigh expedition to Chile during his gap year, 2000

It will get easier as time goes on. Everyone will get bored with me.

> On being the centre of attention when he became an undergraduate at St Andrews University, 2001

F***ing piss off, Postlethwaite.

> To freelance photographer Peter Postlethwaite who attempted to capture him foxhunting, 2002

Prince Harry

The way she got close to people and went for the sort of charities and organizations that everybody else was scared to go near, such as landmines in the third world. She got involved in things that nobody had done before: AIDS for example. She had more guts than anybody else. I want to carry on the things that she didn't quite finish. I have always wanted to, but was too young.

> Remembering his mother on his eighteenth birthday, 2002

The fifth anniversary of her death was important because she wasn't remembered in a way I would have liked.

> On visiting Great Ormond Street children's hospital, one of Diana's favourite charities, 2002

That was a mistake and I learned my lesson. It was never my intention to be that way.

> After being in deep trouble with his father for flirting with drugs and under-age drinking, 2002

You're a f***ing Frog.

> To the French chef of the Rattlebone Inn, Wiltshire, who threw him out for lager-lout behaviour, 2001

The Duke of York

Girls? I like them as much as the next chap.

> Press conference while at school in Canada, 1977

My detective's an excellent fellow, but it's a little uncomfortable to be accompanied everywhere. I sometimes feel like a public monument.

> On the constant presence of a police protection officer, 1980

My only vice is women.

> Interview on joining the Royal Navy, 1980

You've just married my father.

> To the Princess of Wales at her wedding reception, after she had recited Charles's names in the wrong order in her marriage vows and begun with 'Philip', 1981

It simply never occurred to me that because I'm a member of the Royal Family I wouldn't take part if it came to fighting and seeing it through. I was jolly glad that I was here throughout with my squadron.

> On front-line active service as a helicopter pilot in the Falklands conflict, 1982

When you are in your anti-flash gear and are told to hit the deck because the ship is under attack there is nothing worse. You can only lie there and wait and hope. It's a most lonely feeling.

> In the Falklands on board HMS *Invincible*

I saw it [the cargo vessel *Atlantic Conveyor* carrying war supplies] being struck by the missile, and it was something I will never forget. It was horrific. At the same time I saw a 4.5 shell come quite close to us. I saw my ship *Invincible* fire her missiles. Normally I would say it was spectacular, but it was my most frightening moment of the war.

> *Ibid.*

It will be very interesting going back to reality in the UK. It's been one hell of an experience. I suppose I'm not looking forward to going back to being a prince.

> At the end of the Falklands conflict, 1982

Sarah is vivacious, cheerful, outgoing, vibrant. She sparkles, radiating warmth and a sense of fun. There is another word I can use, but I'm not going to say it.

> On his new bride, 1986

She is devastated.

> At an impromptu press conference during the Windsor Castle fire, 1992, on the Queen's reaction to it

You need reasonably good sight to be in the Navy, but as a pilot, once you've flown a bit you can guess the way.

> On leaving the Navy, 2001

If I were to ask you what it is like to be a member of the Royal Family, you wouldn't have a clue. It is just by an accident of birth, a cross we have to bear.

> Interview with *Focus*, armed forces magazine, 2001

I don't wake up at night screaming. It affects people in different ways, I believe. The way to deal with it is called talking about it – better in a pub with your friends than with a counsellor.

> Revisiting the Falklands twenty years on with veterans suffering from post-traumatic stress disorder, 2002

The Duchess of York

He made me eat chocolate profiteroles, which I didn't want to eat at all.

> On meeting Prince Andrew at a dinner at Windsor Castle, 1985. Their romance began when she threw one back at him

A big head who thinks a lot of himself.

> Her first impression of Andrew

I want it to be like something out of Cinderella.

> On plans for her wedding, 1986

Andrew's mother particularly enjoys Ken Bruce and Derek Jameson. She doesn't like the Radio 4 *Today* programme, because she says she has read all the serious stuff in the newspapers.

> On her new mother-in-law's taste in popular Radio 2 presenters

Andrew comes home on Friday absolutely tired out. On Saturday we have a row. On Sunday we make it up but by then he has got to go back to base again.

> On being married to a serving Navy officer, 1987

I'll call it Andrew and hang it on the door.

> Presented with a stuffed buffalo head during a tour of
> Canada, 1987

Last year I learned to fly. This year I'm going to have a
baby. I'm wondering what to do next year.

> Pregnant with Princess Beatrice, 1988

He is my financial adviser.

> On John Bryan, an American businessman secretly
> photographed sucking her toes as she sunbathed topless
> in the south of France, 1992

I had made history all right. I was a failure of historical
proportions.

> On her separation from Andrew, 1992

Whichever girl gets him now is one very lucky girl.

> On her divorce from the Duke of York, 1996

I am easier with myself these days, more forgiving, more
content. I have learned, for example, that there is life after
cellulite.

> *Ibid.*

I will always be the mother of two princesses, and the
second son's ex-wife; there are gossip-page fixtures with
slimmer CVs than that.

> On life after the Royal Family, 1996

We have away games. We play away matches.

> Explaining how she and the Duke of York, divorced but
> still living under the same roof, conduct their respective
> amorous adventures, 1998

Spirituality is like putting petrol in a car. To get the soul
going you have to give it light and energy, and that's spirit.

> Explaining her spiritual nature, 1998

She's a shining little star and I still try to see her as much
as possible.

> On the Queen, who bought her a home of her own, 1999

I've always adored him, but he doesn't have time for me.

> On the Prince of Wales, 1999

He's very frightening.

> On the Duke of Edinburgh, 2001

I will not work in Great Britain. I would be perceived as
using my name and I think that would be about the
rudest thing I could possibly do to Her Majesty.

> Launching her New York-based television chat show,
> 2003

Free your mind and your bottom will follow.

> Her formula for slimming, 2001

He's going to have to come back many lives to sort out that kind of karma.

Condemning the decision by James Hewitt, Diana's former lover, to put their intimate letters up for sale

The Earl of Wessex

I don't think Gordonstoun is as tough as it used to be, but it's certainly an outdoor school, and when you've been living in Scotland for most of the year for five years you get used to a colder climate.

Leaving Gordonstoun with four 'A' levels, 1982

I certainly didn't get a very good degree; it was pretty mediocre. I found revision incredibly tedious. I hope that in the three years I have been here I have done other things.

> Graduating BA from Jesus College, Cambridge, 1986

The Marines are looking forward to having me if only to rub my nose in it. Everybody thinks I'm mad; it's probably the greatest challenge I will ever have to meet.

> Joining the elite and exceedingly tough Royal Marines, 1986

It was a very agonizing decision. Four years ago I wanted to be a Marine. But having got here I changed my mind and decided that the services generally – not just the Royal Marines – was not the career I wanted.

> Abandoning his training after only a year. He went into the theatre instead

I have decided I wish to be other than a member of an elite – any elite. I'm not a Rambo.

> On why the Royal Marines were not for him

It's an experiment, a very radical venture.

> On staging a charity version of *It's A Knockout* (a slapstick television game popular at the time), with members of the Royal Family making fools of themselves as contestants, 1987

I would like the public to view it in a generous way –

130

seeing that members of the Royal Family are, in reality, ordinary human beings.

High hopes before the show

Well, if you can't show more enthusiasm than that …

Storming out of a post-performance press conference, at which reporters had found the contest so embarrassingly awful that they could only shuffle their feet and stare at their boots. The Queen, and the public at large, agreed

It was an experiment and a lot of people have learnt from it. I seem to have lost everything and gained very little.

At least it raised a million pounds for charity

I am delighted with the prospect of joining the company to learn more about the theatre professionally.

On going to work as a backstage dogsbody for Andrew Lloyd Webber's Really Useful Company, 1988

In Britain if you've got a title then you also don't have any brains.

Explaining why he fronted up his film company, Ardent Productions, using the name Edward Windsor, 1998

We are the very best of friends, and that's essential. It also helps that we happen to love each other as well very much.

Announcing his engagement to Sophie Rhys-Jones, 1999

The Countess of Wessex

This has ruined my engagement. This was supposed to be the happiest time of my life.

> On *The Sun* publishing a topless picture of her shortly before her wedding, 1999

I can tell you that he is not gay.

> Defending her husband against persistent rumours, 2001

Horrid, absolutely horrid, horrid, horrid.

> On Cherie Blair, to a *News of the World* reporter posing as an Arab businessman, 2001

The old dear.

> *Ibid*. On the Queen

The Princess Royal

F*** off!

> To photographers who captured her fall at a water jump during horse trials in preparation for the Montreal Olympics, 1976. Since quoted incorrectly as 'Naff off!'

Okay, one says things one regrets. But under the heat of the moment, I mean, one was a very disappointed person at that particular moment in time, and they were all over the place.

Explanation, if not apology, for the above

We fought like cats and dogs. Having an elder brother, I was rather more interested in playing the sort of games that he was playing, rather than anything else. I am delighted that I did not have a sister.

On her childhood with Prince Charles

There is a rather special relationship between the eldest grandson and a grandmother, I think, which is not true of granddaughters.

On the bond between Charles and the Queen Mother

I've always accepted the role of being second in everything from quite an early age. You adopt that position as part of your experience. You start off in life very much a tail-end Charlie, at the back of the line.

On having an elder brother

I don't think a princess is anything I ever played at really. I have probably been playing it ever since.

On her childhood

Noise and smells – that's what school meant to me – cabbage and polish.

Recollections of her schooldays at Benenden

We had two pounds a term, and as I had been brought up by a careful Scots nanny to appreciate the value of money, I simply didn't spend my allotment. I've always been mean with money and as far as I know I was the only girl in the school who had any left at the end of term.

On school pocket money

I gave up hockey as soon as possible and I didn't like netball because I used to get wolf-whistles in my short skirt. I was a bit of a softie and I didn't like rough games.

On school sports at Benenden

I'm afraid I thought it was a grisly waste of time.

On her first riding lesson

It's the one thing that the world can see I can do well that's got nothing whatever to do with my position, or money, or anything else. If I'm good at it, I'm good at it – and not because I'm Princess Anne.

> On an equestrian career that won her a place in the British team at the Montreal Olympics, 1976

I reckon I found the answer in this piece of information pertaining to the Amazons, those formidable forerunners to the women's liberation movement with whom, incidentally, I have no sympathy. They were, apparently, at their most formidable on horseback.

> Her explanation for her equestrian talents

I think it's a very much overrated pastime.

> On why she did not go to university, despite leaving school with six O levels and two A levels

It's difficult to keep the smile bright when you're fourth in line.

> On being criticized for looking glum during a tour of Australia with the Queen, 1970

When I appear in public people expect me to neigh, grind my teeth, paw the ground and swish my tail.

> A victim of her own success as a horsewoman

As a young princess I was a huge disappointment to everyone concerned. It's impractical to go around in life dressed in a long white dress and a crown.

> Recalling her early public life in a TV interview with Brian Walden, 1988

A 19-year-old suddenly being dropped in the middle of the street and being told to go and pick on someone and talk to them. Fun? No, I don't think so.

> Interview, 2002, recalling her first royal walkabout

Princesses are getting a bit short in the market. I'll soon be next, but they'll have a hard job marrying me off to someone I don't want. I'll marry the man I choose, no matter who he is or what he does."

> On press speculation about her marriage prospects, 1968

I can't understand why there has been all this interest in our riding together. Lieutenant Phillips has been coming here solely to exercise the horse he is riding at Badminton, which is stabled here and belongs to the Queen.

On the press noticing that she and Mark Phillips were increasingly in each other's company, 1973

He kept telling me he was a confirmed bachelor and I thought, at least one knows where one stands. I mean, I wasn't thinking about it.

On the announcement of her engagement to Mark Phillips, 1973

I'd prefer a quiet wedding, but the Queen wants Westminster Abbey.

On the wedding arrangements, 1973

There was no reason why Mark should be given a title when we married. He was never going to take part in public duties in his own right, so the question didn't arise.

On her decision that they should be plain Captain and Mrs Phillips, 1973

Having a family can wait a bit longer. I know that some people think you should have your children sooner rather than later, when you are closer in age, but I am not sure. My own family is a splendid example of inconsistency. There was one lot when my mother was very young, and a second lot later on.

On plans for children, 1973

Honestly, three-day eventing at Burghley is a doddle compared to this.

> On giving birth to her first child, Peter, four years later, 1977

At the end of the day, people are always going to refer to him as the grandson of the Queen.

> On her hope that son Peter would be allowed to lead a normal life away from the limelight, 1977

If you stop now, we'll say no more about it.

> To a gunman who stopped her car in the Mall and attempted to kidnap her, 1974

My first reaction was anger. I was furious at this man who was having a tug-of-war with me. He ripped my dress which was a favourite blue velvet I had had made specially to wear away on honeymoon, but of course our main concern was for the people who had tried to save us and who had been shot. They were very brave, and looking back on it now their actions seem even more courageous when you think about them in the cold light of day.

> Inspector James Beaton, her police protection officer, took three bullets, survived, and was awarded the George Cross. Brian McConnell, a journalist who happened to be walking by, won the George Medal for his efforts to dissuade the gunman

The difference now is that when I am on walkabout, I

think and act like a policeman. My eyes are every-where.

> On how the attack affected her

You don't have to love children to save them

> On accepting the presidency of the Save the Children Fund, 1971

It's not for me to pick up a child. It's the people who go and do the work who pick up the children – the nurses, the health workers, the ones who give vaccinations. It's irrelevant whether I pick them up or not.

> On photographers' complaints that she would not pose for the pictures they wanted on visits to Save the Children projects, 1993

She's a great deal better at cuddling children than I am.

> On the Princess of Wales and her different public style, 1994

I didn't match up to the public's idea of a fairy princess in the first place. The Princess of Wales has obviously filled a void in the media's life which I had *not* filled, but I never had any intention of filling it. I had already made a decision that it wasn't me in any way.

> On Diana, the Fairy Princess

That was one of their better fairy stories.

> On media reports that she did not get on with Diana

Whether the media reports my activities, or approves or disapproves, doesn't make any difference to me, although I would obviously appreciate an element of recognition for the many workers that it is my privilege to meet, be they professional or amateur.

> On her treatment by a hostile media, 1986

The AIDS epidemic is a classic own goal by the human race, a self-inflicted wound that only serves to remind *homo sapiens* of their own fallibility.

> Address to a meeting of European health ministers, 1988

Mad cow disease is not a very accurate description of the disease itself, but it is an accurate description of people's response to it. It's not the cows that are mad.

> Backing British beef during the BSE scare at a scientific conference, Edinburgh, 1990

By now I should be used to being misquoted and taken out of context, but in this instance I was particularly irritated. In my position I don't have a political base and I don't attack the Government. It is absurd to say otherwise. There comes a point when you do actually have to say 'Stop', and I am saying it now. So please pay attention.

> Annoyed that she had been reported as taking on Margaret Thatcher's government over the poll tax, and lack of day care for children, 1990

I have seen the pitiful results of each new generation's desire to do something rebellious, and preferably illegal.

Address to the World Drugs Summit, London, 1990

The only thing that stops people behaving badly is the condemnation of their fellow men. We don't do that sufficiently.

BBC Radio interview, suggesting that stern interviews with trained counsellors would have more effect than jail sentences on young offenders, 1990

It is a huge oversimplification to say that all farming ought to be organic, or that there should be no GM foods. I'm sorry, but life isn't that simple. Man has been tinkering with food production and plant development for such a long time that it's a bit cheeky to suddenly get nervous about it when, fundamentally, you are doing much the same thing.

Sideswipe at her pro-organic and anti-GM brother in an interview with *The Grocer* magazine, 2000

Sometimes people get carried away with what they think other people need, but often what people need is not very much – basic facilities, a telephone, a drink, communication, company.

Interview with *The Times* on her role as President of the Missions to Seamen, 2000

Life in general nowadays is more and more isolating. Most people would call it independence, but I'm not sure what that means. It could mean just plain selfish. It could be more convenient just to live all by yourself, but if it means that you don't understand the impact of your life on other people's lives, and how you depend on other people all the time, it's no good. At sea, in a crew, you understand that you can't live alone.

> *Ibid.*

There is a very long list of neglected diseases peculiar to the poor world that are ignored by the research community, which must move up the political agenda. Malaria still kills more children than HIV and AIDS.

> Speech to the British Pharmaceutical Conference, Glasgow, 2001

Humankind is fundamentally idle, and that is one of our real problems.

> Denouncing fast food, 2001

I'm guilty of saying it's only a game. I'll get lynched for that; there are people who think it isn't just a game.

> On high tension over a Scotland–England football play-off for Euro 2000

What a ridiculous thing to do.

> To a wellwisher who had travelled 50 miles to Sandringham to offer her a floral basket, 2000

I never was a fairytale princess. I never was and I never will be.

On herself

Hot pants are the limit. People complain you are not with it, but certain things I will not do.

Declining to succumb to a 1970s fashion

It's always a total mystery to me why I am described as a fashion leader. Clothes are part of the job – if you can call it a job.

But not hot pants

As I get older I'm becoming more adventurous, not only in my clothes but also what I eat.

But still no hot pants

If the press can be so wrong, so trivial and so irresponsible about the Royal Family, the subject I know most about, then they must be wrong, trivial, irresponsible, etc, about everything else.

On hostile media coverage of her

I stand somewhere to the right of Genghis Khan in my attitude to the press. Alfred the Great in the ninth century took a stronger line; persistent slanderers had their tongues cut out.

More of the same

Oh really, why?

> To a journalist who said it was lovely to see her

I did notice my miraculous transformation.

> On coverage of her Save the Children Fund tour of East
> Africa, 1982, when reporters were so short of gossip and
> gaffes to write about that, out of desperation, they decided
> to write about her good works

As President, one of the few things I suppose I can achieve
is publicity.

> But not always the right kind

I feel quite sorry for anyone silly enough to ask me if I
enjoyed my trip. I give them a contemplative look to find
out whether they're genuinely interested, and if it seems
a polite enquiry I simply say 'Yes thank you'.

> On her return from Africa, 1982

Guilty.

> To East Berkshire magistrates at Slough, when asked how
> she pleaded to a charge of keeping a dangerous dog, 2002.
> She was fined £500, and warned that the dog could be
> destroyed if it attacked again

Princess Margaret

I would like it to be known that I have decided not to marry Group Captain Townsend. I have been aware that, subject to renouncing my rights of succession, it might have been possible for me to contract a civil marriage. But, mindful of the Church's teachings that Christian marriage is indissoluble, and conscious of my duty to the Commonwealth, I have resolved to put these considerations before others. I have reached this decision entirely alone, and in doing so I have been strengthened by the unfailing support and devotion of Group Captain Townsend. I am deeply grateful for the concern of all those who have constantly prayed for my happiness.

> Statement announcing her decision not to marry the divorcé Peter Townsend, 1955

Archbishop, you may put your books away: I have made up my mind already.

> To Geoffrey Fisher, Archbishop of Canterbury, who had been searching his library for references on the Church of England's attitude to divorce and remarriage, 1955

My vices are cigarettes and drink. And I don't see myself giving these up.

> Quoted by biographer Nigel Dempster, 1981

I've been misreported and misrepresented since the age of seventeen, and I gave up long ago reading about myself.

> Responding to a *News of the World* interview with her
> lover Roddy Llewellyn, 1980

I adored them because they were poets as well as musicians.

> Her view of the Beatles as the group split up

He never rang or wrote when he was abroad, which made it awkward when friends asked for news of him.

> On her separation from Lord Snowdon after sixteen years
> of marriage, 1976. They divorced two years later

When a 51-year-old woman, the mother of a 20-year old son, puts a 25-year-old ring on her finger, it does not mean she is going to get married.

> Scotching rumours, fuelled by the appearance of a ring on
> her finger, that she was about to marry her current escort,
> the businessman Norman Lonsdale, 1981

I don't know who he is, but he looks like an over-made-up tart. I refuse to be photographed with him; I'm too old for that sort of thing.

> Attending an awards ceremony with the androgynous
> pop singer Boy George, 1982

Princess Michael of Kent

———— ❧ ————

I was unsuitable, quite unsuitable, as a royal bride. I am Catholic and I was also the first tall woman to marry into the Royal Family.

> Looking back on her marriage to Prince Michael of Kent in Vienna, 1978

Marriage is finding someone you can share a flat with.

> *Ibid.* On moving into a ten-roomed apartment at Kensington Palace

I have a better background than anyone else who's married into the Royal Family since the war, excepting Prince Philip.

> *Ibid.* The former Marie-Christine Anne Agnes Hedwig Ida von Reibnitz, daughter of an Austrian count

It is like suddenly discovering you are adopted. Here I am, forty years old, and I discover something that is really quite unpleasant and I shall have to live with it.

> On the disclosure, in 1985, that her father had been a wartime member of the Nazi Party in Austria

The whole key to me is foreignness. But because I talk English like an English person, have English colouring, lead a very English life, people subconsciously expect me to be English in every way. But I'm not; I'm as foreign as could be.

> On herself, born in Karlsbad, Bohemia (now the Czech Republic)

I am very keen on femininity, even though I am six foot and have large bones.

> On her own physique

Tiny boobs and big shoulders.

> Further detail

I may be many things, but I'm not boring.

> Her intellectual self-assessment

They need a soap opera to sell newspapers, and they've got a hell of a soap opera with the Royal Family. They needed a bad girl, and they've cast me in that role.

> On persistent newspaper reports about her haughtiness, and that she freely plagiarised other authors' books when writing her own first work on European princesses

We'll go anywhere for a free meal.

> On criticism that she and her husband were lowering the tone of the Royal Family by agreeing to open a 'Happy Eater' roadside cafeteria

Please don't get up, anyone.

> (Attrib.) On arriving an hour late for dinner with the Queen

He's got my brains, thank heavens, and not the Kents'.

> When their son Lord Frederick Windsor won a place at Eton, 1992

I did not feel my best, but I did not let it show. I kept clutching my red Hermés bag, which matched my red hat and red jacket. Chic colour co-ordination counts, even in an emergency.

> Surviving a helicopter emergency landing in Peru, 2001

What was Said of Royalty

George III

Rather than have granted America her Independence, as my brother-monarch King George has done, I would have fired a pistol at my own head.

> Catherine the Great of Russia's reaction to the news of the loss of the colonies

Queen Victoria

Wit is wasted on the Royal Family, since nothing makes them laugh like hearing one has shut one's finger in the door.

> Lord Granville, Foreign Secretary, on Victoria and Albert's unsophisticated sense of humour

Gladstone treats the Queen like a public department; I treat her like a woman.

> Benjamin Disraeli to Matthew Arnold, 1871

You have heard me called a flatterer, and it is true. Everyone likes flattery and when you come to royalty, you should lay it on with a trowel.

Ibid.

She was wreathed with smiles and, as she tattled, glided about the room like a bird.

Disraeli on his first visit to Victoria at Osborne, 1874

I never deny; I never contradict; I sometimes forget.

Disraeli's secret of handling Victoria

No, it is better not; she would only ask me to take a message to Albert.

Disraeli, asked if he wished a visit from Victoria during his last illness, 1881

Edward VII

Flash'd from his bed, the electric tidings came,
He is not better, he is much the same.

(Attrib.) Alfred Austin's poem 'On the Illness of the Prince of Wales, later Edward VII' during his bout of typhoid fever, 1871. Widely regarded as the worst couplet ever composed by a Poet Laureate

The King has become such an immense personality in England that, as you may have noticed, the space devoted to the movements of Royalty has quintupled since His Majesty came to the throne.

Lord Northcliffe, proprietor of the *Daily Mail*, 1908

It would have been difficult to find any other lady who would have filled the part of friend to King Edward with the same loyalty and discretion.

Lord Hardinge, Viceroy of India, on Edward's long-standing mistress Alice Keppel, 1911

George V

He believed in God, the invincibility of the Royal Navy, and the essential rightness of whatever was British.

The Duke of Windsor on his father

He may be all right as a wise old king ... but for seventeen years he did nothing at all except kill animals and stick in stamps.

George V's official biographer Harold Nicolson on the difficulty of making an entertaining narrative out of his early life, 1952

Edward VIII

Far to the right of even my husband's.

> Diana Mosley, wife of British fascist leader Sir Oswald
> Mosley, on the political views of Edward VIII, 1936

There is no need to lose a single German life in invading
Britain. The Duke and his clever wife will deliver the
goods.

> Rudolf Hess in a letter to Hitler, 1939, on the supposed
> Nazi sympathies of the Windsors

I soon realized that under that delightful smile which
charmed people everywhere, and despite all the fun that
we managed to have, he was a lonely and sad person,
always liable to deep depression.

> Earl Mountbatten on touring with him as a young Prince
> of Wales

There must be men and women on Tyneside, and in
Liverpool and South Wales, who are remembering
today the slight, rather shy figure, who came briefly into
their lives, and sometimes into their homes, in those
grim years ... I have no doubt that the Duke by his
conduct as Prince of Wales and as King has paved the
way to a form of monarchy which today is more in tune

with the times than would have been thought possible fifty years ago.

> Prime minister Edward Heath in the House of Commons on the death of the Duke of Windsor, 1972

Queen Elizabeth the Queen Mother

She never has a bet herself but, my goodness, she devours the *Racing Post*.

> Racing manager Sir Michael Oswald on the Queen Mother, 2000

My hatchet is buried, my venom dissipated. I am glad to salute a remarkable old lady. Long may she live to be the pride of her family. And may God understand and forgive me if I have been ensnared and corrupted, if only briefly, by this superb royal trouper.

> William Hamilton, Labour MP and lifelong anti-monarchist campaigner, on the Queen Mother's eightieth birthday, 1980

During her long and extraordinary life her grace, her sense of duty and her remarkable zest for life made her loved and admired.

> Tony Blair, Prime Minister, on the death of the Queen Mother, 2002

You stood with your husband as he was confronted with kingship. It was, in your own words, an intolerable honour.

> George Carey, former Archbishop of Canterbury, at the Queen Mother's centenary service, 2000

Of all the members of the Royal Family, she was the one who had the surest common touch in dealing with people.

> Alex Salmond, former leader of the Scottish National Party, on the death of the Queen Mother, 2002

One of the reasons she was so popular was that she never gave interviews. The last time was in 1923, and she was rapped on the knuckles. She never did it again.

> Andrew Roberts, historian, on the Queen Mother, 2002

We are witnessing the passing of the last eminent Victorian – something we won't see again for many decades.

> Sky News commentator on the Queen Mother's funeral, 2002

The answer, if you ask me, is that the Queen Mum has a reputation for liking her drop of gin. Everyone loves a granny, but a granny on the razzle is irresistible.

> Keith Waterhouse, playwright, explaining the Queen Mother's popularity, 1999

She was not fond of black folk, but these are of course traits typical of her age and class.

> Journalist Paul Callan reviewing her life, 2002

The Queen

She Queen is entitled to use the gifts that God has given her to mimic anyone she pleases.

> The Rev Ian Paisley, on hearing that the Queen did a wickedly accurate impersonation of him, 1998

She has become a parrot.

> Same author, same subject, but different context, 1998

She was neat.

> President George W. Bush on meeting the Queen, 2001

Your Majesty, everyone wants a pound of your flesh.

> Nelson Mandela to the Queen on her visit to South Africa, 1999

She grins and bears it.

> Sir Elton John, rehearsing for the Golden Jubilee pop concert, 2002, on the Queen's attitude to rock music

I think one of her deepest secrets is that she finds us all faintly ridiculous.

> Robert Lacey, royal biographer, on the Queen's attitude to her public, 2002

The great thing about talking to the Queen is that everything is totally confidential. Apart from my wife, she's the only other person in the world that you can say something to and know it will never go beyond the bounds of the room.

> Tony Blair on his weekly audience with the Monarch, 2002

Since Your Majesty's visit to the Vatican, our nation has passed through difficult times.

> Message to the Queen from the fiercely anti-Catholic Free Presbyterian Church of Scotland blaming her audience with the Pope for a spate of train crashes, floods and an epidemic of foot-and-mouth disease, 2001

It's like the NSPCC having a paedophile as its patron.

> A senior official of the RSPCA on having the pro-foxhunting Queen as patron, 2001

The Queen is a very pleasant middle to upper-class type of lady with a talkative, retired Navy husband.

> Malcolm Muggeridge, anti-monarchist, 1957

The personality conveyed by the utterances which are put into her mouth is that of a priggish schoolgirl, captain of the hockey team, a prefect, and a recent candidate for Confirmation. It is not thus that she will be enabled to come into her own as an independent and distinctive character.

> Lord Altrincham (historian John Grigg) on the Queen's style of public speaking, 1957

It says much for the Queen that she has not been incapacitated for her job by woefully inadequate training.

> *Ibid.*

She does not enjoy 'society'. She likes her horses. But she loves her duty and means to be a Queen and not a puppet.

> Harold Macmillan, Prime Minister 1957–63

What one gets is friendliness, not friendship.

> James Callaghan, Prime Minister 1976–79, on his weekly audiences with the Queen

I do not think anyone fully realizes the accumulation of experience she has.

> Margaret Thatcher, Prime Minister 1979–90, on the Queen

The Queen does not notice what other people are wearing.

> Buckingham Palace official to Margaret Thatcher, who

had apologized for arriving at her first weekly audience dressed identically to the Queen, 1979

One's Bum Year

Headline in *The Sun* on the Queen's *'annus horribilis'* speech, 1992

At one time I got quite anxious about Lilibet and her fads. She became almost too methodical and tidy. She would hop out of bed several times a night to get her shoes quite straight, her clothes arranged just so.

Marion Crawford, former royal nanny, in *The Little Princesses*, 1950

The Queen's relationship to God changes as she moves over the Scottish border. She becomes less important.

Andrew Duncan in *The Reality of Monarchy*, 1970. Although Supreme Governor of the Church of England, she is a mere member of the Church of Scotland

Elizabeth had been seven when her father had acquired the first of these stumpy, bad-tempered beasts for which she would develop an almost comical soft spot.

Robert Lacey on the Queen and her corgis in his biography *Royal*, 2002

Elizabeth II is not an actress. At the heart of Britain's performing monarchy is a serious, matter-of-fact woman who is an obstinately performance-free zone.

Ibid.

Not in my garden.

> The Queen to Sir Paul McCartney, who asked if she would be repeating the successful Golden Jubilee rock concert, 2002

Why does one have wax in one's ears?

> The Queen while touring a London medical school, 2002. None of the trainee doctors could tell her

The poison that Diana faced did not come from the Queen. Her Majesty is not capable of hurting people. Diana knew that when she died; the Queen was not one of her enemies. There was never any hatred between the two of them.

> Paul Burrell, former royal butler, in the *Daily Mirror*, 2002

The Queen came through for me. I'm thrilled.

> *Ibid*. Burrell's trial collapsed after the Queen remembered a conversation she had had with Burrell

I have a great admiration for her as a person. I danced with her in 1945 when I was 19, and I once won her in a raffle.

> Tony Benn, veteran left-wing politician, on the Queen, 2002

In her youth the Queen was quite a stunner. Who knows what might have happened if I'd met her at Tramp in my heyday.

> George Best, one-time star footballer and reformed alcoholic, 2002

It was lovely talking to her, especially as I am a Windsor too.

> Barbara Windsor, TV soap star, on receiving her MBE from the Queen, 2000

What's your name?

> Sol Masters, aged three, to the Queen when she visited his Australian nursery school, 2000

There is no way the Queen and Paul Burrell stood for three hours chewing the fat; thirty minutes would have been a bloody miracle.

> An unnamed courtier on Burrell's claim that he had talked at great length to the Queen about Diana

The Duke of Edinburgh

The Duke of Edinburgh is a national treasure.

> Editorial in *The Times* after his latest gaffe, 2002

I hear you're trying to invent something like the Hitler Youth.

> Education minister David Eccles to Prince Philip on his plan to launch the Duke of Edinburgh's Award Scheme, 1956

An unreconstructed racist . . . arrogant, ignorant and a waste of time.

> Kumar Murshid, race relations adviser to London mayor Ken Livingstone, on the Duke of Edinburgh, 2000

We may be scum, sir, but we are the *crème de la scum*.

> Veteran journalist Harry Arnold to the Duke of Edinburgh, who had berated a group of reporters at Sandringham

The Great Wally of China

> Headline in the *Daily Mirror* on the Duke of Edinburgh's celebrated 'slit-eyed' remark during the state visit to Beijing, 1986

Philip Gets It Wong

> Ditto, *The Sun*

The Prince of Wales

Duchess would be too grand. Lady too common. Countess is the perfect compromise.

> Buckingham Palace courtier speculating on what title Camilla Parker Bowles might be given if she married the Prince of Wales

You speak good sense and someone should make you king one day.

> Boris Johnson, Conservative MP and editor of *The Spectator*, praising the Prince of Wales's views on the countryside, 2001

I thought he was one of the saddest men I had ever met.

> Penny Junor, biographer of the Prince of Wales, 1999

It's a shame we can't all live at Highgrove. Nobody is forced to buy our houses, but they do.

> Housebuilders George Wimpey rebutting the Prince of Wales's attack on modern housing developments, 1999

Oops, Charles! There's a Patch on Your Thatch.

> *The Sun* reporting the Prince of Wales's thinning hair, 1977

Decades of exposure and effort may bestow a shadow of 'charisma' on some exceptional figures like John Lennon or Bob Dylan. Prince Charles, alas, unfairly acquired the real thing merely by being born.

> Tom Nairn in his political polemic *The Enchanted Glass: Britain and its Monarchy*, 1988

There is room, in these enlightened times, to accept Charles's irregular love life for what it is – an accident of history – and to tolerate its continued existence.

> Christopher Wilson in *A Greater Love: Charles and Camilla*, 1994

I'd suffer anything for you. That's love. It's the strength of love.

> Camilla Parker Bowles to Charles in the 'Camillagate' taped telephone conversation, 1993

The amount of kit and servants he takes around is grotesque.

> (Attrib.) The Queen, on the Prince of Wales and his staff of more than eighty, 2002

Diana, Princess of Wales

Princess Diana polled twice as many votes as Charles Darwin. Obviously we have a lot more evolving to do.

> Letter to *The Times* on the BBC Television series *Great Britons*, 2002

What a cunning lady. This one is clearly going to give us a lot of trouble.

> James Whitaker of the *Daily Mirror* who, on being the first journalist to spot the Prince of Wales and Lady Diana Spencer together, noticed that she was watching him in the mirror of her powder compact, 1980

I hope that when people look back, they'll see Diana's influence on the monarchy as a positive one.

> Earl Spencer on the fourth anniversary of his sister's death, 2001

The Spencers found Diana unacceptable in life. But after her death they found her very acceptable at £10.50 a ticket.

> Paul Burrell, former royal butler, in the *Daily Mirror*, 2002. On the Althorp museum

She was the people's princess.

> Prime Minister Tony Blair on the morning after her death, 1997

Prince William

He is not an institution, nor a soap star, nor a football hero. He is a child.

> Lord Wakeham, chairman of the Press Complaints Commission, warning the media not to intrude on Prince William during his time at Eton

I am a realist. I do not believe it possible or desirable to prohibit newspapers entirely from speculation and reports about young ladies who might become a more permanent feature of his life.

> Lord Wakeham again, as Prince William prepared to enter St Andrews University

I'm a drug addict, not a paedophile.

> 'It' girl Tara Palmer-Tomkinson denying reports that

she had slept with Prince William while he was still at
school

He became bored and fed up, and that made him rather
lonely.

Prince William's spokeswoman on reports that he was
unhappy at St Andrews University

This row about Prince William being filmed going into
lectures would never have happened in my day. Art
students never went to lectures.

A former undergraduate commenting on the Earl of
Wessex's film crew which outstayed its welcome on
Prince William's first day at university

He has asked that people do not call him sir or bow when
they meet him.

Advice from Prince William's spokeswoman to fellow-
students at St Andrews University.

He did the hand movements but not the dance routine.

A hotel-owner who observed Prince William's karaoke
version of Village People's hit, *YMCA*

Prince Harry

The job of protection officers is to protect the princes, not mother them.

> Prince Harry's spokeswoman on why his police escort did not step in to stop his cannabis smoking and teenage drinking

The Duke of York

You will forgive me, won't you, my royal gorgeousness?

> Television presenter Cilla Black after mistakenly introducing the Duke of York as the Duke of Edinburgh, 1999

It's a common misapprehension that all he does is play golf.

> Buckingham Palace spokesman defending the Duke of York, 1998

You may be a prince, but I am a queen.

> Sir Elton John, rock musician, to the Duke of York, 2001

The Duchess of York

The Coronation Street princess.

> Princess Michael of Kent on the Duchess of York, 1986

This may not be full-blooded infidelity, but toe-kissing and bare-breasted embrace does imply a level of intimacy beyond the normal bounds of financial advice.

> Henry Porter, *Evening Standard* columnist, on the pictures of the Duchess of York with her financial adviser John Bryan, 1992

The Countess of Wessex

Sophie is bright. She is attractive. But royal she ain't.

> James Whitaker, royal reporter, on the Countess of Wessex, 2001

The Princess Royal

————

She saw the police car and believed it was waiting to escort her on her journey.

> Solicitors for the Princess Royal, charged with speeding, explaining why she was driving at 93 mph with a patrol car in hot pursuit, 2001

The key to the princess is that she is Prince Philip in skirts.

> Lady Colin Campbell in *The Royal Marriages*, 1993

Princess Anne has to be one of the most charmless women I have ever come across.

> Penny Junor, royal biographer, 2001

Scurrilous, absurd and without foundation.

> Buckingham Palace statement following press reports that the Princess Royal's marriage to Captain Mark Phillips had broken down and that she was having an affair with the Queen's equerry, Commander Tim Laurence, 1989

Princess Margaret

————

The ashtray.

> Waiter at London's Mirabelle restaurant, asked what was

the favourite dish of Princess Margaret, a regular customer

Even her friends are obliged to address her as 'Ma'am' or, if especially close, as 'Ma'am Darling'.

Biographer Theo Aronson on Princess Margaret, 1997

Ultimately, duty has demanded of Princess Margaret rather more than privilege has restored.

Her semi-official biographer Christopher Warwick, 1983

She was coquettish, sophisticated. But what ultimately made Princess Margaret so attractive and lovable was that behind that facade, the apparent self-assurance, you could find, if you looked for it, a rare softness and sincerity.

Group Captain Peter Townsend on his former lover

She was far too bright for her station in life.

Gore Vidal, author, on the death of Princess Margaret, 2002

Princess Margaret is very, very, very frightening, but beautiful and succulent, like Belgian buns.

Sir John Betjeman, former Poet Laureate

One hep chick.

> Louis Armstrong, jazz legend, on meeting Princess
> Margaret

Princess Michael of Kent

Far too grand for the likes of us.

> The Queen on Princess Michael of Kent, 1978

Princess Alexandra

My mother is a total hypocrite. When it counted, she wasn't there for me. This is the dark side of the Royal Family; the other side of the postcard is for the tourists.

> Marina Ogilvy, daughter of Princess Alexandra,
> claiming her parents gave her an ultimatum of abortion
> or shotgun marriage when she found herself pregnant,
> 1990

The Monarchy

They cannot talk about modernization but hide under ancient old rules when it suits them to cover up on money.

> Alan Williams, Labour MP, on Buckingham Palace's refusal to disclose details of the Queen Mother's will, 2002

As long as people continue to bow to an uncultivated woman, the caste system will continue.

> Actress Claire Bloom on the Queen, 2002

The real question that absorbs everyone is: who is sleeping with whom. All roads inexorably lead to or from the royal bedchamber.

> Lady Colin Campbell in *The Royal Marriages*, 1993

My passport's green.
No glass of ours was ever raised
To toast The Queen.

> Irish poet Seamus Heaney objecting to being included in an anthology of contemporary British poetry, 1983

It happens all the time. Spink's jewellery department has had many royal belongings coming in over the years either from Kensington Palace or elsewhere. It wasn't just servants, though, who brought them in. Members of the Royal Family themselves would come into us and sell items.

> Stephen Dix, former director of a London auction house, on reports that Royals sold off unwanted gifts for cash, 2002

I don't want a bicycling monarchy, just a pottering one.

> Keith Waterhouse, playwright, 2000

You don't manhandle the monarchy – unless you are a policeman.

> Buckingham Palace spokesman after the Princess Royal had been touched on the arm by an official in Sydney, 2000

The institution of monarchy is inherently silly. And it obliges everyone it touches to do silly things.

> Lord Hattersley, Labour peer, 1998

The royals are far more human than people give them credit for.

> Rory Bremner, impressionist, 1998

The institution of monarchy is well past its sell-by date. Without the monarchy we could have an open society, an open constitution.

> Lord Rothermere, proprietor of the *Daily Mail*, 1998

The last thing we need is a New Monarchy, like New Labour.

Lord Tebbit, Conservative peer, 1997

Having a hereditary monarchy is like having a hereditary rugby team.

Paul Flynn, Labour MP, 1997

I became a monarchist when I saw people curtsying to Mrs Thatcher. I thought, 'God, that's dangerous. Let's have something safe like the monarchy.'

Doris Lessing, novelist, 2002

The monarchy allows us to take a holiday from reason, and on that holiday we do no harm.

Martin Amis, novelist, 2002

I belong to the band of fairly unshakeable monarchists, but I sustain my faith by never wanting to meet any of the Royal Family.

A.N. Wilson, writer and columnist, 2002